A Brighton Tragedy

Bell's Indian and Colonial Library.

A BRIGHTON TRAGEDY

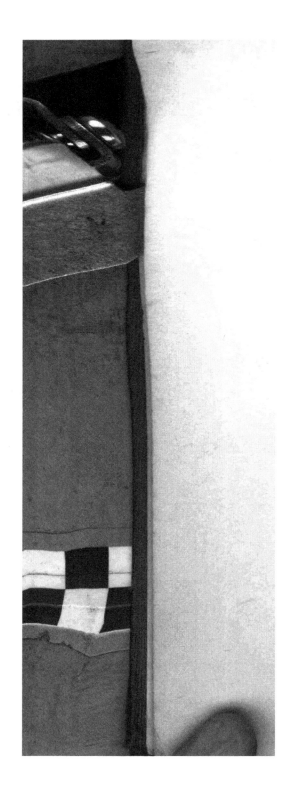

A Brighton Tragedy

By Guy Boothby

Author of
"Dr. Nikola," "A Desperate Conspiracy,
"A Consummate Scoundrel,"
Etc., etc., etc.

London
George Bell & Sons
1905

This Edition is issued for circulation in India and the Colonies only.

CONTENTS

A BRIGHTON TRAGEDY

A BRIGHTON TRAGEDY

CHAPTER I

THEY represented two distinct types of humanity
—the Englishman and the Spanish-American.
Each had his own racial peculiarities, yet in one
or two particulars they were curiously alike. They
differed in this way. The Englishman was tall,
spare, slow of speech, and modest to a degree
that bordered on the absurd. The Spaniard was
of medium height, somewhat fleshy, voluble in
speech, and as vain as the proverbial peacock.
Yet both were reckless, both were courageous,
both were good fighters, and both were ready to
take their own parts and to maintain them on
the slightest provocation. In addition to this both
were what the world calls rolling stones, and so
far neither of them appeared to have gathered
much moss in the course of his journey down the
hillside of Life. They had been more or less

acquainted for several years, but had never been anything further—friendship between them was impossible. There were several reasons to account for this—but as the narration of that will fall into its proper place there is no need for me to speak of it now.

The Englishman's name was Anstruther—Eric Anstruther. He was the cadet of a fine old Yorkshire house, well endowed with brains but cursed with a craving for a roving life. Educated at Eton, he had sucked in all that that venerable seat of learning could teach him in the way of athletics — and but little more. His career at Oxford was rendered famous by many interviews, of a more or less painful nature, with the authorities of his college, ending, as all such things do end, in his being compelled to quit the University at remarkably short notice, much to the disgust and anger of his sorely-tried father, which anger was not lessened when the sum total of his son's debts was placed before him. The old gentleman was the possessor of a scathing tongue, and he made use of it to some effect on this occasion.

" It seems I have been the means of bringing a fool into the world," he remarked, as he placed the sheet of paper on his study writing-table.

To which his son respectfully replied, " We must all make mistakes at times, my dear father."

From that moment forward both felt that the gulf between them was unbridgeable. A cheque for two hundred pounds was handed to him, and the young man was ordered to leave the house forthwith and forbidden under penalty ever to show his face there again. At first he tried South Africa—but without success; next he crossed to Chili, and to his intense delight arrived in time to assist in an abortive revolution. When that reached the conclusion that anyone with any claim to common sense might have predicted for it, he turned his attention to Brazil, to presently find himself on the verge of starvation in the streets of Rio. Brazil proving of no use to him he continued his journey north, eventually finding himself in the Republic of Colombia—one of the most remarkable places on this planet, if I may be permitted to say so. To recite its history would take too long, even if it were in keeping with this narrative, which it is not. Let it suffice, therefore, that it was once an empire second only to that of the Incas of Peru and the Aztecs of Mexico. It was captured by the Spaniards in 1537, and then it was that it received the magic name of El Dorado.

After many vicissitudes, Anstruther at last reached the capital—Bogotá—a town of upwards of a hundred thousand inhabitants, perched on a vast plateau some eight to nine thousand feet above sea level. Here Fortune at last began to shine upon him. When, at his wits end to know what he should do to keep body and soul together, he chanced to render a signal service to a wealthy merchant of the city, who to that business added another of ranch owner. Being as hospitable as he was wealthy the latter insisted on the young Englishman accompanying him to his house, some fifteen miles from the city, and becoming his guest there until such time as he should decide what he intended doing. Nothing loth, the young man consented, and they accordingly set off. Don Miguel D'Araugo's country residence was about as charming a home as the heart of man could desire. The lady of the house was an ideal hostess, while she was ably seconded in her endeavours by her daughter, Donna Catalina—then but little more than sixteen years of age, although, as is usually the case with Spanish-Americans, she looked at least two years older. As it soon transpired, they were great admirers of England and the English, and in consequence they offered a hearty welcome to the young man whom the father had invited to be their guest. The result must be obvious to the meanest intelligence. One cannot ride day after day with a lovely girl in the early morning, before the sun has begun to throw long shafts of light over the mountain-tops, or listen to her singing to the accompaniment of her guitar, in the cool *patio,* flooded by moonlight, without feeling some touch of the tenderest of all tender passions. At least, Eric Anstruther could not ! By the time he had been a fortnight at the *hacienda* Santa Barbara he was over head and ears in love. And small wonder, for Donna Catalina was the loveliest girl, not only in Bogotá, but probably in all the Republic of Colombia. As I have already said, she looked older than she really was. For one so young she possessed a matchless figure : her hands and feet were the tiniest imaginable, her hair was black as the raven's wing, her eyes were dark and lustrous, and if, perhaps, her complexion had a tinge of olive in it—it only served to accentuate her other and more varied attractions. She was a consummate and daring horsewoman, a good shot with a rifle, and, since a fault must be found to balance so much perfection, about as ignorant a young lady, so far as book learning was concerned, as could have been discovered between Cape Horn and the Isthmus of Panama.

" What does it matter ? " her father was wont to ask when his wife spoke to him on the subject. " She will learn all that is necessary for her to know in good time. She is but young yet. Later on we will take her to Europe and have her taught everything in order that she may develop into an artificial society humbug without a natural side to her character. Come, come, wife, you know as well as I do that you would not have her otherwise than she is—innocent as a lamb, honest as the blue sky above us—and better than all a loving and affectionate daughter to her parents. What more could any father wish for ? "

After which harangue he would go off in search of his daughter to tell her that her mother wished to send her away to school in Europe, at which threat she would laugh, knowing that such a thing would never happen. Fate, however, is not infrequently stronger than either our beliefs or our

expectations, as I shall endeavour presently to
show. "*Voll Weisheit sind des Schickals Fügun-
gen,*" says old Schiller, the philosopher, and I
suppose we must believe him.

Just as Anstruther was debating in his own mind
as to whether he was justified in remaining longer
at Santa Barbara, and at the same time wondering
what he should do when he left it, Don D'Araugo
came to him with a proposal of such magnitude
that it almost took his breath away. It appeared
from what he said that the assistant manager of
his great cattle farm of San Pedro, one of the
largest in the Republic, had died somewhat suddenly, and he now offered Anstruther the vacant
post, and at a salary which, at the time, it must be
admitted, was more than commensurate with either
his deserts or his experience. Situated as he was,
I need not say that he hastened to accept, and with
real gratitude. All he regretted was the fact that
it would involve his leaving Santa Barbara, and
with Santa Barbara—Catalina. So far she had
not heard the news, and it fell to his lot to have
to break it to her.

It was a perfect moonlight night, and they were
seated together in the *patio*, she with her guitar,
upon which she had been playing—and he with
the more prosaic cigarette between his lips. The
fountain splashed musically, the silver rays of the
moon just catching the jet as it reached its height
and commenced to descend gracefully into the pool
below. Pleased as he was at finding employment,
Anstruther had nevertheless been unusually silent

all the evening. Doubtless Donna Catalina found him so, for she rallied him upon it in English, which, by the way, she spoke with a barely perceptible Spanish accent. The curious phrasing of some of her sentences was a source of never-ending delight to Anstruther.

"How is it now?" she said, when they had been seated together for some time. "I think you are very sad to-night. Perhaps I have offended you, but I am innocent of knowing in what way."

"You, Senorita?" he answered, as if with some surprise. "You could not offend me if you tried! What should make you think that I am sad? But for one thing, I am happier, I think, than I have ever been in my life before. You know that!"

"And what is that one thing?" she enquired, ignoring the last sentence. "Will you not tell me? You but yesterday said that you looked upon me as your true friend, and you promised that you would tell me all your troubles. You are now sad, and yet you will not let me know what makes you so. It is not kind. Believe me, I do not like it."

She drew herself away from him as if her dignity were offended by his lack of candour.

"But I am not in trouble," he answered; "at least, not in the way that you imagine. I am only sad—but what does it matter? I suppose I shall get over it."

Her voice was very soft and low as she replied, "But it does matter. I do not like you to be sad

—you are always so happy. Can you not confide
in me? When my father is worried by anything
he tells me all his trouble and I do my best to
cheer him up. Come, I insist upon knowing what
it is that has made you so cast down."

" But you may not be pleased when you hear,"
he returned. " It is more than possible that it
will offend you."

She placed her guitar upon the coping of the
fountain and then turned to Anstruther ; her white
slender hands were clasped upon her knees.

" You said just now," she continued, " that it
was not in my power to offend you—what, therefore, if I return the compliment? You cannot
offend me. There, I have said it. Now go on ! "

To give himself time to think how he should
break the news to her, Anstruther very slowly lit
another cigarette. He began to wish that the
subject had not cropped up at all. She was little
more than a child, and, whatever his own feelings
towards her might be, it was scarcely fair to put
ideas into her head that could never by any chance
be realised. He was man of the world enough to
know how quickly such seeds are apt to germinate
and how big a tree may spring from the smallest
of beginnings. And yet, cast about him as he
would, he could discover no other adequate excuse
to account for the feeling of despondency which
had taken possession of him. One thing, however, was quite certain, and that was the fact that
she was growing every moment more and more
impatient with him. She had never seen him in

this mood before, and she resented it as being almost a slight to herself. Her curiosity was also piqued.

" The fact of the matter is," he said at last, " I am unhappy because the time has come for me to bring my visit here to a close. I have been so happy that I cannot bear to think I must leave Santa Barbara and my kind friends."

There was a look of absolute dismay upon her beautiful young face as he said this that should have been flattering to his vanity—had he possessed any. But he was not in the humour to be flattered, and he was far from being vain. That had been knocked out of him long since. He was thinking how different his life would be on that far-away cattle farm, remote from civilisation of any sort—his only companions the roughest of the rough, and his lodging the mockery of a home. And worse than all, there would be no Catalina to ride with him, to wander with him in the quaint old-world garden, or in the evening to sing tender little Spanish songs to the accompaniment of her guitar and the splashing of the fountain in the *patio*. It would be a change with a vengeance and, so far as he was concerned, not for the better. And yet he knew that he should be grateful for the chance it offered him of earning his livelihood.

" You are going away?" she said at last. " Ah! I see, you are tired of us. You find that existence at Santa Barbara is too quiet for you. You want to go out into the great world again,

B

to live the life you have so often told me of.
Well, I am sorry, but I suppose we cannot blame
you. You have the right to do as you please.
We shall all miss you very much. I think you
know that—my father especially.''

There was something very near akin to a sob
in her voice as she said this. It cut into Anstruther's heart like a knife. He felt that, if he
were not very careful, he should lose control over
himself and say things he should regret ever
after.

'' I am afraid you do not quite understand,'' he
said hurriedly, for he began to fear that she was
about to burst into tears. Remember, she was
little more than a child. '' When I say that I
am going away I mean that I am going to San
Pedro. Your kind father has offered me the
assistant managership of the farm, and I am to
take up my duties at once. It is a great chance
for me, and I am more than grateful to him for
it. At the same time, I cannot disguise the fact,
even if I wanted to, that I am very sorry to leave
Santa Barbara, where I have been so happy.''

'' You are going to San Pedro?'' she exclaimed.
'' But it is such a long way off! And from what
I have heard from my father, it is such a rough
place.''

'' I am accustomed to roughing it,'' Anstruther
replied, with a bitter laugh. '' For the last few
years my life has been spent in just such places—
though I am afraid the luxury I have known here
will make it rather strange and a little unwelcome

at first. However, I have no doubt I shall soon shake down and look back on the last few weeks as being part of some beautiful dream that was too good to last."

He paused for a moment. His heart was beating wildly within him, and the words which he knew he had no right to utter trembled on the tip of his tongue. She looked so beautiful, lying back in her long cane chair, that the temptation to tell her of his love was increased a hundredfold. Never in his life, and he had met many beautiful women in his perambulation of the world, had he seen one who could compare with her—and if she were so beautiful now, what would she be in two or three years' time? Then came the bitter thought—all the more bitter perhaps because he was only too well aware that he was powerless to prevent it—that some other and more eligible suitor might win her hand. For probably the first time since he had been turned out of the old Yorkshire home he regretted the folly which had brought that disastrous event about.

"Senorita," he said at last, leaning a little nearer her and speaking in a voice which trembled with emotion, "when I am gone you will think of me sometimes? We have been very happy together."

"Of course I shall think of you—and often," was her reply. It was evident that she did not catch his real meaning. "I shall do so every day. You will find, when you come back from San Pedro, that I have not forgotten you. How could I?"

There was an ocean of flattery in that last query, and he took it to his heart and hugged it close to comfort himself. The mere remembrance of it was destined to warm his blood through many a long day and dreary night when on the plains with the cattle. It was evident now, for the time being at least, he had forgotten that he was only her father's servant — a grade above the ordinary *Llaneros,* or cattle men — it is true — but not so very far removed after all. He heaved a heavy sigh—which the girl misinterpreted, as it was only natural that she should do. She thought he sighed because he was so lonely in the world. It was a curious circumstance, but nevertheless a fact that he had never spoken to her of his home-life.

" Have you no one who cares for you ? " she asked, with gentle sympathy, after the silence which followed her last speech.

" Not a soul," he replied. " My mother died when I was a boy—my father would rather kill himself than recognise me, and my only brother follows his example. No ! I am quite alone in the world. It may seem selfish to say so, but that is why I value your sympathy so highly, and also why I have been so happy here. You, in your peaceful home-life—surrounded by all that love can bestow, can have no idea how desolate I am. And the most galling part of it all is the knowledge that I have only myself to thank for it. But I don't know why I am talking like this. I'm like a hysterical schoolgirl."

" You're nothing of the kind," she answered

indignantly, " —and oh, I'm so sorry for you. But I cannot help wishing that you were not going to San Pedro. It is such a long way away, and there is no one there who will be a companion to you."

"There is the manager, Señor Bartolomé Quintana," said Anstruther.

"You will not like him, I am sure of that," she answered decisively. "I cannot bear him— though my father considers him a very clever man. He frightens me every time I look at him—with his coal-black eyes that seem to pierce one through and through. There have been some terrible stories told of him and his brutality to the *peones* —but my father declares that they are not true; that they have been invented by his enemies in order to discredit him in his eyes. But I am not so sure of that. I believe him to be capable of anything. I pray of you, whatever else you do, not to quarrel with him. Your life would be unbearable if you did. He would never forget, and he would never forgive."

"I am not likely to quarrel with him," Anstruther replied. "In the first place, I shall be his subordinate, and in the second I am not of a quarrelsome nature. I have no doubt we shall manage to hit it off together somehow."

"I pray that you may," said she, with great earnestness, "for I confess to you that I myself are more afraid of him than I am of any other living man."

"I trust you are not afraid of me," laughed

Anstruther. "But there, perhaps you do not consider me a very terrible person."

"I am not going to tell you what I think of you," she answered. "But I do want you to take the warning I have given you seriously to heart—for, believe me, it is not an idle one."

"I will promise to do so," he returned gravely. "And I thank you for giving it to me. As our English proverb has it, 'Fore-warned is fore-armed.' I will do my best to get on amicably with the worthy Señor Quintana, if only to earn your good opinion."

At that moment her mother entered the *patio* with the news that it was bed-time. Their *tête-à-tête* was at an end.

Next day Don Miguel and Anstruther had a long and confidential chat together concerning the young man's new employment. He gave the latter a variety of good advice, and at last touched upon the subject concerning which his daughter had spoken to Anstruther on the previous evening —namely, his association with the manager of the ranch, Señor Bartolomé Quintana.

"I don't disguise from you the fact that he is a somewhat difficult person to get on with," he observed. "But, after all, the Devil is not as black as he's painted—nor do I believe Quintana to be. As you will soon discover for yourself, he has a rough and turbulent crew to control, and at times it is vitally necessary that he should rule them with a rod of iron. I must confess that there have been occasions when I have not altogether approved of his methods—but I have been wise enough not to interfere so long as it did not go too far. With your experience of the world you must know that no good ever comes by backing the fo'c'sle against the after-guard. I hope, for both your sakes, you will be able to manage to get on well together, and I will pay you the compliment of saying that I feel sure it will not be your fault if you do not."

Eric thanked him for this expression of his good opinion, which he was determined he would do his best to deserve. Next morning he prepared to depart. He bade his host and hostess farewell, and thanked them from the bottom of his heart for the kindness they had shown him. But Donna Catalina was not present to bid him " Godspeed," and her absence puzzled him considerably. Why did she wish to avoid him? Had he offended her on the previous night, or was she so sorry at his going that she did not feel equal to saying " Good-bye? " He did not know what to think of it. It was not like her to treat him in this fashion. Though he felt hurt, he did his best not to show it.

" Will you bid the Señorita ' good-bye ' for me? " he said to his hostess, "—and thank her for her goodness to me. I am sorry not to have an opportunity of doing so in person."

" Where is the child? " asked her father.

The mother only shook her head—she was not going to commit herself on the subject of her wayward daughter's actions.

At last Anstruther mounted his horse, a
driving the mule, which carried his bagga
before him, set off on his long journey. On
old Spanish bridge which spans the river a qua
of a mile or so from the house, he stopped, a
turning in his saddle, looked back. Still th
was no sign of Catalina. Five minutes later
had turned the side of the hill and the *hacie*
had disappeared from view. The old Span
causeway—deep with dust—lay before him, n
upon mile, with the mountains rising on eit
side of the valley through which it passed.

He was thinking of the happy time he t
spent during the last few weeks, and was wond
ing how long a period would elapse before
should see the place again, when there was
rattling of stones on the hillside above him, a
next moment Donna Catalina made her appe
ance, mounted on her young thoroughb
" Mazeppa," and pulled him back almost on
haunches within a yard of the edge of the ba

" Did you think that I would let you go with
saying ' good-bye ' ? " she cried, and the you
man thought he had never seen her look
beautiful as she did at that moment. " Ah
can see you did. But see, here I am. I ha
been watching for you from the hillside."

" It is kind of you to come," he answered.
had begun to despair of seeing you, Señorita.
shall never forget your kindness to me."

As he said this the handkerchief she held
her hand was caught by the breeze, and by so

strange chance was blown in his direction. Urging his horse forward, he caught it and once more looked up at her, laughing as he did so.

"I shall keep it to bring me luck," he cried, and thrust it into his pocket.

"How foolish you are," she said, but her eyes told him that she was not displeased at his action.

A few moments later he was jogging along on his way once more, and she was only a speck upon the hillside.

Little did either of them dream under what circumstances they next would meet.

CHAPTER II

In due course, that is to say, at the end of five days' journey, Eric Anstruther reached the cattle farm of San Pedro. It was towards evening when he emerged from the primeval forest through which he had been travelling for the past three days and found himself on a vast open plain, dotted here and there with clumps of dainty *moriches*—a specimen of palm valuable for the roofing of huts and possessing a peculiarly graceful appearance. A large number of cattle were grazing on this plain, but though the guide which Anstruther had brought with him declared that the *hacienda* of San Pedro itself was not far distant, he could discern no trace of it. When, however, they had proceeded some two or three miles further, the thatched roofs of the little settlement came into view. The Ranch House itself was picturesquely situated on the right bank of a swift flowing stream, which, fed as it was from the mountains, never ran dry at any season of

26

the year. It was surrounded by the various farm buildings, including the stock-yard—the branding pens and the *peones'* huts. From a distance it presented a by no means unpleasing appearance, but closer inspection rather destroyed the gilt on the gingerbread. The buildings for the greater part had fallen to decay, even including the manager's own residence, into which, as the new arrival was to learn before very long, the rain streamed as through a sieve in the wet season.

As soon as they sighted their destination, Anstruther and the guide pushed forward at increased speed. After so many camps in the dense forest, the former was more than anxious to be safely housed under a roof once more. In addition he was desirous of getting his first interview with Quintana over and done with as soon as possible. He felt that he should not rest easy in his mind until that ceremony was a thing of the past. When, however, he reached the little cluster of buildings and dismounted from his horse, at what might be described, with a little exaggeration, as the manager's front door, it was only to learn from the mulatto woman who kept house for him — a gruff and somewhat sinister person — that Quintana was not at home; that, as a matter of fact, he had gone on a visit to a *hacienda* some forty miles distant and was not expected back for some days. Anstruther then explained who he was and, having handed his horse to a *peone*, unshipped his baggage, and entered the house that was destined to be his home for many a long and weary month to come.

If the outside of the house was in a dilapidated condition the inside more than matched it. The living-room, which opened into the verandah, if by such a term the covered-in space which surrounded the building might be described, was of fair size. The walls and ceiling had once been lined with canvas, but this was now perished beyond all hope of repair, and in many places hung in long strips which fluttered and rustled unceasingly under the influence of every breeze that entered through the ever-open windows. The floor, which was of earth, beaten hard, had worn into many holes, some as much as three inches deep. To be in keeping with everything else, the furniture was of the most primitive description, and consisted of a rough table which showed evident signs of having been home-made—three chairs with the same trade-mark upon them—a rough cupboard, constructed from a packing-case —a coloured portrait of the famous Liberator— Simon Bolivar—another of Garibaldi, and more incongruous than all, an oleograph of the child Samuel praying in the Temple. From the living-room opened two bedrooms, each as scantily or perhaps more scantily furnished than the other.

"You can have this," grunted the mulatto woman, indicating with a nod of her head the apartment on the right.

Anstruther eyed it with evident disfavour. After

the daintiness and luxury to which he had for the
last few weeks been accustomed, it looked scarcely
better than a third-rate dog kennel.   However,
such as it was, it behoved him to make the best
of it, so he settled himself in with as good a
grace as he could muster up, cheered always by
the remembrance of a lovely girl seated on a
thoroughbred horse looking down on him from
the mountain-side.   How many times during the
next few days he took that precious handkerchief
from his pocket in order to examine it—it would
be impossible for me to say, nor, being a crusty
old bachelor, can I imagine what satisfaction he
derived from the performance.   That there must
have been something pleasing to him in the ceremony was evident from the expression upon his
face as he replaced it on each occasion in the
pocket whence he had taken it.

By the time Quintana returned to the ranch,
Anstruther had made himself quite familiar with
it and its workings, and had also put himself on
good terms with the hands employed.   They were
a rough and turbulent crew, but generous and
warm-hearted in the main, as is usually the case
with men whose lives are spent in the open air
and the wild life of the great plains.   Tough as
whipcord, they scarcely understood what fatigue
meant, but could sit in the saddle from sunrise to
sunset, in the broiling heat of summer, or the
piercing cold of winter, without so much as a
murmur of discontent.   The sky as often as not

was their roof, the hard earth their bed, and their diet the simplest of all simple foods known to man.

It was late in the afternoon of the fourth day after Anstruther's arrival at San Pedro that Quintana put in an appearance. The former had returned from a ride half an hour or so before, and was now stretched out in a hammock in the verandah, thinking of Santa Barbara, and of Catalina you may be sure. Suddenly his ear caught the sound of horse's hoofs on the hard-beaten track which led up to the house. He raised himself to a sitting posture in order to find out who the newcomer might be. For a moment he could not see anyone—then a man on horseback turned the corner of the house and pulled his animal up exactly opposite where Anstruther was seated. He presented a picturesque appearance and one thoroughly characteristic of the country. He was a man of about thirty-two years of age— apparently of medium height, though it was difficult to judge accurately when he was seated in the saddle. His face was dark and swarthy—yet by no means unhandsome. A heavy moustache covered his mouth, and from the way in which it was curled, it was evident that its possessor set no small store by it. His eyes were dark as sloes, and had a peculiar expression in them that spoke for a temper that could not always be kept under control. He was dressed in the fashion of the Plains—that is to say, he wore a broad-brimmed sombrero, a poncho enveloped his shoulders, while his legs were incased in *zamorros*, or leggings, of tanned hide with the hair left on, and lined with soft leather. His saddle was of the Spanish-American pattern—high at the back, much ornamented with brass-headed nails, and having for stirrups large shoes of burnished copper, in which the whole foot is enclosed. On the pommel was curled his lasso of twisted hide, without which no cattle man would dream of travelling even the shortest distance. Large and heavy silver spurs decorated his heels and gave a finishing touch to an already sufficiently picturesque personality. The animal he bestrode was a well-bred beast, and the possessor, so Anstruther discovered later, of a temper that could only be fitly described as being as fiendish as that of its master. On this occasion, however, she appeared to have no fight left in her, so furious had been the pace at which the forty miles had been traversed. She was covered from head to foot with foam, and when she came to a standstill her drooping head and heaving flanks seemed to say, " I admit that whatever victories I may have won before, I have been fairly and squarely beaten to-day."

On seeing the newcomer, Anstruther turned out of his hammock and went forward to greet him. Though he had never met him before, he felt quite certain in his own mind that he was Quintana —his superior, and the man against whom he had been warned. Anxious as he was to get on well

with him, he had to confess to himself that he
was not prepossessed by first appearances. He
told himself that the other looked exactly what
Catalina had declared him to be—a braggart and
a bully. At the same time, he argued that it was
scarcely fair to judge so soon; it behoved him
rather to keep his mind quite free from all bias
until he got to know him better.

"Unless I am mistaken, you are Señor Quintana," he said in Spanish as he approached the
horseman.

The man curled his moustache and admitted
that he was the individual in question—and then
enquired whom he was addressing.

"I have come from Don Miguel D'Araugo,"
Anstruther replied. "I have a letter from him
to you. He has been kind enough to give me the
position of under-manager on this ranch."

The other's face did not betray any signs of
satisfaction on hearing this. As a matter of fact
he had looked forward to appointing one of the
hands already upon the place, a tool of his own,
to the vacant position—and it displeased him to
think that his intentions had been forestalled in
this fashion, and by an Englishman too of all
people in the world. However, he was too clever
to allow the other to see that he was annoyed, so
he dismounted from his horse, and held out his
hand with the friendliest air possible.

"I am delighted to have the honour of making
your acquaintance, Señor," he said. "I have no

doubt that we shall work most amicably together. I offer you my apologies for not having been at home to receive you on your arrival."

Though his words were civility itself, there was a curious note of insincerity underlying them that Anstruther did not at all like. He was not going to allow the man to suspect this, however. He had no doubt that, with the exercise of a little diplomacy, they would settle down together in time and manage to rub along in a fairly amicable fashion, even if they could not actually be friends.

The first six months of Anstruther's life upon the ranch were not altogether months of unalloyed happiness. The work was in a measure strange to him, while his home-life—if by such a title it could be dignified—was of the most comfortless description imaginable. With the exception of their work, he and Quintana had not an idea in common, while there were a hundred and one subjects upon which they differed. The manager was possessed of that peculiarly irritating faculty of being able to make himself disagreeable without actually saying anything offensive. Times out of number the younger man was on the verge of quarrelling with him, but on each occasion he remembered the promise he had given to Catalina, and managed to control himself in time to avoid open rupture.

When Anstruther had been at San Pedro a year, Quintana began to throw out hints to the effect that he thought himself entitled to a holiday.

C

The idea gradually grew upon him until one day, a fortnight or so after the annual *rodeo*,—or round-up of the cattle and the consequent branding operations—he announced his intention of leaving the ranch and setting off for Bogotá and civilisation on the morrow. Anstruther was to be left in charge.

" I'm afraid you won't have a very lively time of it, my dear friend," observed Quintana, and added with a sneer: " Still, you will have the satisfaction, so dear to every Englishman, of knowing that you are doing your duty. Was it not one of your great statesmen who told his compatriots that England expected every man to do that? I cannot help thinking I have read it somewhere. It seems to me a pity that they should have sunk to such a depth as to stand in need of a reminder."

That was the man's way exactly.

Next morning soon after daybreak Quintana saddled his horse and, taking a pack animal with him, set off on his journey. Before he left, however, he enquired whether he could deliver any message for the other at Santa Barbara, where he proposed spending a few days on his way to the capital. He was anxious, so he said, to renew his acquaintance with the pretty Señorita Catalina, whom he declared he had worshipped ever since she was a child.

" She was adorable then—she must be doubly so now," he remarked; " and what is more, she will one day be one of the wealthiest women in this country. I wonder you did not try your luck in that direction, Anstruther, or perhaps you were generous enough to leave her for me. If so, I thank you, and will promise you to make the most of my opportunities." Here he curled his moustache and leered at the other until the latter felt that, if he continued to talk in this strain, he should lose his temper and knock him down. Quintana saw that his arrow had hit the mark, and the thought pleased him. He mounted his horse and rode off laughing. " Friend Anstruther is in love," he said to himself as he cantered down the track. "But for that matter, so am I—or at least, I intend to be. He had better not interfere with my plans or it will be the worse for him. Four million dollars are worth fighting for, and, at the old fellow's death, she will be worth that if she's worth a *centavo*. No, no! *amigo mio*, don't you come between me and my ambition— Bartolomé Quintana can be friendly enough when it's necessary, but he is a dangerous man to play with, and, worse than all, to make an enemy of."

With these amiable thoughts in his mind he plunged into the forest and for the time being gave no thought to the man he had left behind him.

To say that Anstruther's life was a dull one after Quintana had departed would be to describe it very mildly. There was literally nothing for him to do. The round-up was over, and with it the one excitement of the year had come to a conclusion. Day after day he read, smoked, ate and slept, varying matters now and again when a chance wayfarer made his appearance in search of his hospitality. But even these gentry were few and far between, and, as often as not, they were of a class that could only be relegated to the men's huts.

Six weeks later Quintana returned. Anstruther was sitting on the corals, or stockyard fence, watching the breaking of a fiery colt at the moment that he spied him crossing the plain. As he drew nearer, he descended from his perch and advanced to meet him. He had been so lonely that, much as he disliked the other, he was almost eager to welcome him back.

" Glad to see you," he said, holding out his hand. " I hope you have had a pleasant holiday."

" A very pleasant one," the other replied, " if it were not spoilt by this cursed return to exile. It's that that kills all the enjoyment. Hi ! Pedro —Gomez—you lazy rascals, come and take these horses and bring my baggage up to the house when you have attended to them. What's more, keep your fingers out of the traps, or I can promise you you'll hear from me. Now, Anstruther, come along. I'm starving for a drink, and I want to hear how things have been going on in my absence."

He said this as if he doubted whether they could have prospered at all. It was evident that he had not reached home in the best of tempers. Once more Anstruther felt the necessity of keeping himself well in hand. His solitude during the last few weeks had rather put him out of practice, and it behoved him now to re-learn the lesson he had taught himself with as little delay as possible.

On entering it, Quintana looked round their living-room with evident disgust.

"A pig-stye," he muttered; "only fit for a hog to live in."

He mixed himself a double quantity of *aguardiente* as he spoke, and pushed the bottle across the table towards his subordinate, who poured himself out a small quantity, more for the sake of politeness than for any other reason.

"Here's to fortune," he said; "and if you like we will combine with it the health of the Señorita Catalina, whose devoted slave I am and always shall be."

They drank the toast without any remark on the younger man's part. He saw that the other hoped he would say something, but he was resolved not to be drawn. Quintana mixed himself another glass, stronger than the first, and then seated himself in a chair beside the table.

"I stayed at Santa Barbara," he remarked, "both going and coming, and everyone was most kind—the Señorita in particular."

"The Señorita is kindness itself to *all* with whom she is brought in contact," said Anstruther,

with a marked emphasis upon the "all." "I
hope Don Miguel and his wife are well?"

The other did not answer this question, perhaps
he did not hear it. That he had noticed the sig-
nificance of the first portion of the young man's
speech was apparent, however, from the heavy
frown that wrinkled his forehead. He would have
retaliated in kind had he been able to think of a
speech that would have been sufficiently cutting.
As it was, he had to let it pass, and his subordinate
chuckled inwardly as he noticed it. For once he
had scored.

"And now tell me what has been going on
here," said Quintana, abruptly changing the subject. "I have given you all my news and you
have as yet told me nothing."

"There is very little to tell. You know what
the life is like after the annual round-up. There
is plenty of water and plenty of grass, and the
cattle seem to be doing all that is required of
them. A jaguar killed two beasts out on the third
cañon three weeks ago."

"I hope you killed him."

"Judge for yourself," said Anstruther, pointing
to a fine skin upon the floor. "There is his hide."

"Any trouble with the hands?"

"None at all. I had no reason to make trouble
with them."

The manager uttered a scornful laugh. The
spirit he had drunk was fast taking possession of

him, and he was ready to find fault with anything or anybody.

"I suppose I shall find them as slack as the deuce," he said. "I never did and I never shall believe in petting men, specially these vermin."

"I am not aware that I have been petting them," retorted Anstruther angrily. "The men are rough, it is true, but they are willing enough if they are properly handled."

"By that, I presume, you mean that I don't handle them properly," continued the other. "If you think so, why haven't you the pluck to say it? I can take my own part as well as any man, if I don't happen to be an English gentleman. I can hold my own with men *and women,* as you may have occasion to find out before very long, Mistaire Anstruther—and don't you forget it."

"I am not going to dispute your assertion," Anstruther replied, "and for the simple reason that I do not think it worth while."

"*Dios y Demonios!* But you shall think it worth while," cried Quintana in a paroxysm of rage at the snub. "I have put up with too much of your infernal conceit, and I don't intend to do so any longer. I have treated you too well in the past and you have taken advantage of it."

In another moment Anstruther would have lost his temper altogether, but he was saved by the appearance of Gomez, who had brought Quintana's baggage up to the house and now placed it on the floor of the living-room. The latter cursed him for having been so long about it, and bade him carry it into his bedroom, whence he himself staggered a few minutes later.

Anstruther threw after him a look of profound disgust, and then, in his turn, entered his own apartment. Presently Gomez re-appeared and, seeing no one in the living-room and believing that the manager was occupied with his unpacking, thought it a fitting opportunity to help himself from the bottle of spirit on the table. He had poured out a glassful and was raising it to his lips when Quintana appeared in his doorway and saw what he was doing. Advancing on him, he struck him a tremendous blow behind the left ear. The man went down as if he had been shot, and the glass was broken into a thousand fragments.

" Get up, you cur," cried the manager, and kicked the prostrate body savagely.

This was more than Anstruther could stand.

" Touch that man again," he cried, " and I'll break every bone in your body."

The other tried to answer him, but his wits failed him, and, turning on his heel, he staggered back to his room.. As he disappeared, Gomez re-covered consciousness and sat up. Anstruther gave him something to drink and in a few minutes he was able to get on to his feet. He shook his fist in the direction of Quintana's door.

" Wait, wait," he muttered. " This is not the first time, and Gomez will not forget."

Then, swallowing what remained of the liquor,

he left the house, and Anstruther passed into the verandah.

When the mulatto woman came to inform him that the evening meal was served, he felt half inclined to say that he did not want any, for he had no desire to quarrel again with the drunken bully who was his chief; but the latter, it appeared, was fast asleep, so he took his accustomed place at the table and was about to fall to work, when something stopped him. Beside his plate lay a large envelope with his name upon it, in Don Miguel's handwriting. Quintana had evidently brought it. Wondering what it could contain, he opened it, to find inside three letters. The first was from the Don himself, and merely expressed his satisfaction at the manner in which he had performed his duties, combined with the hope that, before very long, it would be possible for him to pay them another visit. The second was in a handwriting that set his heart beating like a sledge-hammer. It was from Catalina—a frank, girlish epistle, brimming over with friendliness. She told him all the news of Santa Barbara, and echoed her father's wish that it would not be long before they saw him again. Though there was really nothing in it, the infatuated young man read and re-read it until he almost knew it by heart. Then, and not till then, did he take up the third envelope. It bore an English stamp and a London postmark —but who it was from he had not the least idea. It ran as follows :—

Lincoln's Inn Fields,
25th July, 1904.

DEAR SIR,

It is with the most profound regret that we find it necessary to inform you of the lamentable decease of your respected father and brother, Messrs. Augustus and William Anstruther—which sad event was occasioned by the disastrous railway accident which occurred on Friday last on the London, Becksfield and Marborough Railway. The terrible nature of the catastrophe has, as doubtless you know, cast a gloom over the entire country.

The estate being strictly entailed, the reversion, of course, passes to you, and we hasten to place ourselves at your disposal—presuming that you would wish us to act for you as we have done for your father and grandfather before you. Presupposing that you will deem it advisable to return to this country without delay, and not knowing how you may be situated with regard to ready-money, we take occasion to enclose herewith a draft on the Anglo-Colombian Bank for the sum of £500.

Assuring you always of our best attention,

We remain,

Obediently yours,

TOLSON, MATTHEWS & DURNFORD.

For upwards of five minutes Anstruther sat staring at the paper before him.

"Both dead," he muttered; "and my father gone without forgiving me."

Then another thought occurred to him.

"My life here is at an end," he said. "I will leave to-morrow morning for Santa Barbara—and, if she will have me, Catalina shall be my wife."

CHAPTER III

AT break of day next morning Anstruther was up and about. He had much to do in order to get ready for his journey to the capital. So far he was scarcely able to realise the importance of the change that had taken place in his fortunes. It must not be considered heartless on his part that he did not betray greater grief on hearing the news of the death of his father and brother. Of course, he was genuinely shocked by the sad intelligence, but in his favour it must be remembered that neither of the dead men had ever attempted to make his home-life a happy one. He had been looked upon, with more or less justice—on that point I am not prepared to venture an opinion, as the scapegrace of the family, and he had been treated as such. Without wishing to speak ill of the dead, I can only say from personal knowledge that both were hard, narrow-minded men, primed with their own conceit and totally incapable of making allowances for the

44

shortcomings of others. The old gentleman had turned him out of house and home for what was, after all, little more than a mere boyish indiscretion, and one which happens sooner or later in almost every family that sends it sons to either University. It is scarcely to be wondered at, therefore, if he were not as overwhelmed with sorrow as he might otherwise have been.

Having arranged about his horses, he returned to the house to find Quintana in the living-room, mixing himself his *mañana,* or "morning greeting," of *aguardiente.* It soon became evident that the latter was ashamed of his behaviour on the previous evening, or at least for as much as he could remember of it. As proof of this, he greeted Anstruther with a cordiality such as he had never exhibited towards him before.

"I'm afraid I was not quite what I might have been towards you last night," he began apologetically. "I ask your pardon for it. Let us try to forget it. It must have been the coming back to this dismal hole that put me in such a bad temper."

He pressed the bottle on Anstruther, but the other declined the invitation. He was wondering how he should break the news of his intended departure to the manager. That the latter would not be best pleased by it he knew beforehand.

"You received your letters, I suppose?" said Quintana at last. "I told Tina to place them on the supper-table for you."

"Yes, I received them," Anstruther replied, "and it is about one of them that I want to talk to you."

"Go ahead then, my friend," continued the other, rolling a cigarette as he spoke. "I hope it is nothing worrying, for I am not feeling in the humour for anything very serious this morning."

He lit the cigarette and leant back in his chair.

"Well," said Anstruther, "the fact of the matter is, among the letters Don Miguel forwarded to me by you, there was a communication from my English lawyers informing me of the death of my father and brother, who were killed in a railway accident some three months ago."

"Permit me to offer you my condolences," replied the other, blowing a dainty cloud of smoke through his nose as he spoke. "May I ask if it will make any important difference in your affairs?"

"It will make all the difference in the world to me," Anstruther answered. "Instead of being a poor man, I shall be worth between six and eight thousand a year."

"You are indeed to be congratulated," sneered Quintana, who was overflowing with envy. "I presume you will now abandon Colombia to her fate and return to England to enter upon your inheritance?"

"That is my intention," the younger man said quietly. "I wanted to let you know that I shall be leaving here in two hours' time. That it is rather short notice I am well aware, but I have so much to do before I leave for the coast that I cannot afford any delay."

Quintana stole a glance at him under lowering brows. His suspicions were aroused, and he thought he could understand what the other meant when he said he had so much to do. In consequence, his rage sprang up like a squall on a mountain lake, and in a sense it was equally dangerous. He controlled his voice sufficiently, however, to ask whether the other proposed visiting Santa Barbara on his way to the capital.

"I shall probably make it my headquarters while I am there," Anstruther replied unsuspiciously. "Don Miguel has been kind enough to invite me to be his guest."

The other man ground his teeth in impotent fury, for he did not see how he was to prevent his rival from taking advantage of the situation, which, as will be seen, was all in his favour. He had learnt while at Santa Barbara, something of the state of things which had existed between Catalina and Anstruther, and the memory of it rankled in his mind continually. What would the consequences be now when that man, young, rich, handsome, and the possessor of a fine estate, should present himself in the capacity of a suitor for the Señorita's hand? The result would be almost a foregone conclusion. And yet the other did not see how he was to stop it. For the moment the thought of accompanying Anstruther occurred to him, but he immediately saw the impossibility as well as the unwisdom of adopting such a course. Yet he was determined not to give in without a struggle. He had long made up his mind to obtain possession of Catalina, and, what was more important, the large fortune which would some day be hers, and he told himself that it would fare ill with the man who should endeavour to baulk him of his prey. He would follow him, if necessary, to the end of the world, in order to be revenged. And what was more, he had others, who, for the sake of the money at stake, would help him. These thoughts, although they have taken me some time to set down, in reality flashed through his brain at lightning speed. The expression of his face meanwhile was far from being a pretty one. It was the expression of a man who would do and dare anything to attain the object on which he had set his heart.

"Well, since you have made up your mind to go," he said at last, "I suppose I cannot prevent you. At the same time, I must say I think you're playing it rather low down on me in leaving me in the lurch like this."

"I don't see that at all," replied the other. "You as good as told me last night that I was of no use to you, and what is more, you have your *protégé* Sebastian at your back. Let him take my place. You would have given it to him before, had not Don Miguel appointed me."

Quintana looked up at him quickly. He had

no idea that the other knew anything of his intention to promote Sebastian to the position. If Anstruther had discovered this, how much more did he know? There was a certain little matter not unconnected with the sale by private treaty of some of his employer's stock that he had no desire should reach that gentleman's ears, at any rate, not until he, Quintana, was safely out of the country. Colombian jails, under the happiest auspices, are far from being pleasant abiding places, and more especially so when the convict happens to have entertained the idea of marrying his prosecutor's daughter. But Quintana proved equal to the occasion, as he usually did. There was a smile upon his sallow face, and his manner was as unconcerned as ever it was as he replied, " So you know of that, do you? Well, you must do me the credit of admitting that I did not do it. Don Miguel forestalled me, and perhaps, all things considered, it was as well that he did. Sebastian is a good enough man, but, after all, he is too much in touch with the other hands to be altogether reliable. You say you want to get away in two hours; in that case you had better tell Tina to prepare you a meal as quickly as possible. It will be the last decent one you will have until you reach the *venta* at Santa Maria."

He spoke so pleasantly that Anstruther, with characteristic generosity, began to repent of having lost his temper with him. Little did he guess the tempest that was raging in the other's breast, nor had he any idea of the murderous thoughts that

D

were filling his brain. Had he done so he would assuredly have been more on his guard. As it was, though for the time they had been together they had been practically at daggers drawn, they parted the best of friends and with what appeared to be mutual regret. Thus may a clever and unscrupulous villain hoodwink and bamboozle one whose only claim to consideration is his honesty and singleness of purpose.

"I wonder if I have misjudged the fellow after all," said Anstruther to himself, as he made his way across the plain towards the forest through which he was to travel for the next few days. He would have been amply satisfied on this point if he had heard the other's remark as he watched him go—"You think you've beaten me, do you? Just wait and see. I think I can promise you you'll be surprised before I'm done with you. You haven't won Catalina yet, and it won't be my fault if you ever do."

For the next half-hour he sat at the table, scowling at the world in general, and trying to discover some way in which he could rid himself of the young man who had just left him. That young gentleman, meanwhile, was riding on his way through the forest in as happy a frame of mind as anyone you could have found in the continent of America. His exile at San Pedro was at an end, and he was on his way to the girl he loved, and who he sincerely hoped loved him in return. Over and over again he rehearsed the meeting. Would time have changed her, or would she be the same witching, impulsive maid that he remembered so well of old? He did not want her to be different in any single particular. She had been perfect then, and he argued that any change could only be for the worse.

Perhaps it may have been his impatience to reach his destination that made the journey appear so long, but it seemed a veritable eternity before he turned the side of the hill and saw the *hacienda,* bathed in sunlight, lying in the valley before him. How home-like it looked, the grey walls and red-tiled roofs, the luscious green meadows surrounding it, and the rocky torrent of the little river dashing along behind the cluster of farm buildings of which their owner was so justly proud. It was in every sense of the word a delightful home, and, after the discomfort and squalor to which he had for so long perforce been accustomed, it struck Anstruther as being little short of an earthly Paradise. As soon as he saw it he urged his tired horses forward, and, in less than ten minutes, had drawn up before the great gates of the house. He dismounted and rang the bell. In response to his summonses old Diaz, the major-domo of the household, made his appearance and threw open the portals. At first glance he did not recognise the bronzed *zamorro* clad young man before him, but as soon as the other spoke, he cried, " It is Señor Anstruther, and to think that I did not know you, blind old mole that I am. Blessed be the Saints; but his Excellency and the ladies will be right pleased to see you."

" Not more pleased than I shall be to see them,"
Anstruther replied, in all sincerity. Then the old
man called to one of the grooms, who happened
to be passing at the moment, and bade him take
the horses, himself unstrapping the baggage and
carrying it into the house. In the *patio*, where
the fountain still played as of old, reclining in a
silken hammock with a book and revealing the
daintiest pair of ankles imaginable, was no less a
person than Catalina herself. The splashing of
the fountain prevented her hearing his entrance,
so that he was permitted an opportunity of gazing
at her without her knowing that he was doing so.
And what a picture it was to set before an impressionable young man who was already over
head and ears in love with the original. If Catalina had been lovely when he had last seen her,
she was a hundred times more so now. The girlish
air had almost, if not quite, departed, and in its
place was the bewitching dawn of womanhood of
which poets have sung since time immemorial.
Delightful as the picture was, he could restrain
himself no longer, but advanced boldly towards
her. She looked up on hearing his step, paused
for a moment as if in amazement, and then, with
a glad little cry, slid from the hammock and advanced with both hands outstretched to meet him.
" Oh, I am so glad to see you," she said. " I
began to think you would never come back to us
again." Then, for the first time, she must have
realised that he was still holding her hands in his,
and that he was gazing into her face with an

ardour that was scarcely compatible with her maidenly dignity. She blushed and hung her head. Then she tried to draw her hands away from him, but he would not let them go. "Catalina," he said, and it was the first time he had called her by her Christian name without the customary prefix, "you are more beautiful than ever, and I don't care in the least how angry you may be with me for saying so. You don't know how I have longed for this moment. When I received your letter I felt as if I should know no peace until I saw you again."

"Perhaps I ought not to have written," she observed, pretending to take a vast interest in the gold fish disporting themselves in the basin of the fountain. "Some people might consider it a most unmaidenly proceeding on my part."

"Then some people are idiots of the first water," he replied scornfully, "and consequently their opinions are not worth the consideration of sensible folk. I would not part with that letter for a King's Ransom."

"I am afraid you have grown very foolish during your stay at San Pedro," she retorted. "But here am I keeping you talking when you must be both hot and tired after your long ride. My father has gone into the city, but my mother is at home, and I know how glad she will be to see you. Let me take you to her."

Anstruther followed her to Donna D'Araugo's favourite room, where they found her seated at the window, working as usual at her interminable embroidery. She had, perhaps, grown a little greyer, but the welcome she offered the young man was as sincere, though less demonstrative, as that he had received from her daughter. Then she called for Diaz and bade him conduct Señor Anstruther to his old apartment, whence he emerged half an hour later, clad in civilised garb and looking the very picture of a cleanly, well-groomed, young Englishman. Don Miguel had returned by this time and echoed the welcome that had been given him by his wife and daughter. He enquired after the cattle farm, but for some reason best known to himself, said nothing with regard to Quintana. This rather puzzled Anstruther, but he was destined to receive enlightenment later on. From what he was informed then, he gathered that Quintana had occupied himself with making violent love to Catalina during his stay at Santa Barbara—much to the disgust of that young lady and her father. He had pushed matters to such extremes at last that the Don had been compelled to interfere and to ask the gentleman to find lodging elsewhere, much to his discomfiture. Anstruther was able now to understand something of the reason that had brought the manager back to the ranch. Needless to say he had not mentioned the matter to his subordinate—but knowing what we do now, his jealousy and hatred of the younger man is to be easily accounted for.

That evening Anstruther informed Don Miguel

of the change that had taken place in his fortunes, and went on to tell him that, in consequence, it would be necessary for him to resign the appointment the other had given him, and for which he had been and always should be grateful.

" I shall be sorry to lose you," replied the Don, " but I can quite see that you have other claims upon you now which must come before everything else. When do you propose leaving for England, for I suppose you intend going home ? "

" I shall leave by the next boat," Anstruther answered. " She calls at Cartagena on the thirteenth of next month."

" And after that you will go away into the great world and forget all about us," continued the worthy old merchant with a laugh, " for I do not suppose we shall ever see you again."

" I am never likely to forget you," replied the young man indignantly, " and it will not be my fault if we do not see a great deal of each other. I shall look forward to entertaining you in England before very long. It is only fair that you should give me an opportunity of returning the generous hospitality you have shown me out here."

But the elder man shook his head sadly.

" I shall never see England again," he answered. " I have long had a strange presentiment that—that—" he paused, as if he did not quite know how to express himself. There was a look of intense pain upon his face that Anstruther did not understand.

"May I ask what form that presentiment takes?" he enquired, thinking it might do the other good to talk about it, for there could be no doubt that he was disturbed in his mind about something.

"I scarcely like to tell you," replied the old gentleman. "It is a subject upon which I am particularly sensitive. However, I think, my dear lad, that I shall be quite safe in confiding in you."

"You may be perfectly sure, sir, that whatever you tell me will go no further," said Anstruther. "I should have too much respect for the confidence you place in me."

"I will trust you," he said. "The fact of the matter is, I am, and always have been, a superstitious man. It was born in me, I suppose; at any rate, its power has influenced my entire life, ofttimes for good, but sometimes for evil. For a longer time than I care to think about I have been haunted by the belief that this particular year is destined to prove fatal to me—in other words, that it will be the last I shall see."

He paused and wiped his forehead with his pocket-handkerchief. Anstruther gazed at him in complete astonishment. Was it possible that this strong, hard-headed man of business could believe in such things? For a moment he scarcely knew what to say. It was plain that to attempt to reason with him would be only so much waste of time.

"Do you really mean to say that you believe your life to be in danger?" he asked at last, as

if the very thought of such a thing were incredible
to him. " Surely you cannot believe that ? "

" I do most firmly and implicitly believe it,"
was the other's reply. " And what is more, I
am as certain as I can well be of anything, that I
shall not die in my bed."

" Good Heavens, sir ! " cried Anstruther, " you
must not give way to such morbid thoughts as
these. Think of your wife and daughter."

The old gentleman rose and began to pace the
room excitedly, his hands clasped behind his back.

" It is of them I am thinking always—and more
particularly of Catalina. My warning tells me
that her mother will not long survive me, and
what will become of her when both are gone I
dare not think. I have an old friend in England
who has visited me here on several occasions—
perhaps I could induce him to take care of her,
though it would be putting his friendship to a
rather unfair test."

" May I ask his name ? "

" His name is Tolson—he is a solicitor."

Anstruther nearly jumped out of his chair in
his excitement.

" You surely don't mean George Bramwell
Tolson, the head of the firm of Tolson, Matthews
and Durnford, of Lincoln's Inn Fields ? "

" The same man," answered the other. " Do
you happen to know him ? "

" I have known him ever since I was a boy,"
was Anstruther's reply. " He is our family

solicitor, and one of the kindliest men living. Know old Tolson, as we disrespectfully used to call him?—I should think I did. Why, I have a letter from him at this moment in my pocket."

As he spoke he took from his pocket the letter in question, and handed it to the Don.

" There is the hand of Fate in this," he heard D'Araugo mutter. Then turning to the other, he cried, " You could not have given me better news. I think I can pin my faith on Tolson."

" I am certain of it," said the younger man, " but I feel assured that you will never have to do so. Your life is as good as mine."

" Time will show," replied D'Araugo.

That night Catalina and Anstruther sat, as they had so often done before, in the *patio*. Again it was moonlight, and again the mellow light touched the dancing waters of the fountain. He told her for the first time, for he had had no opportunity of doing so before, of his accession to fortune, and of all that it meant to him.

" And you are leaving Colombia and returning to England? " she said, with what was almost a gasp.

" I must do so," he replied. " I have to see my lawyer concerning the estate."

" And will you ever return? " asked the girl.

" That depends," he answered.

" Upon what? "

" Upon you," he replied.

" But how can it depend upon me? " she asked, and he noticed that her voice trembled as she said it.

" Because you know as well as I do that I love you, and that, without you, the world is nothing to me. Will you be my wife, Catalina ? "

She had been frightened, but she was not so any longer. She gave him her hand.

" I have loved you from the first," she said, and in this simple fashion the matter was settled between them.

Half an hour later Anstruther had a second interview with the Don. The latter's delight at the news was only equalled by his own.

" I had hoped that this would happen," he cried.

" And you give your consent ? "

" I do, and with every blessing on you both. But, and I am afraid this may cause you some disappointment, I must ask you to give me your word that you will not make her your wife until she has reached her twentieth year."

" But that will be two years to wait," groaned the young man.

" Never fear, they will pass quickly enough. Will you give me the promise ? "

" If you really wish it, I suppose I must."

His wife, when she heard of it, echoed his good wishes, and it was a happy household that retired to rest that night.

The next three days were days of unalloyed bliss to the betrothed pair. They rode and walked together, and seemed incapable of remaining long out of each other's sight. The Don was as pleased as they were, and declared that, if it were not for the important speech that he had to make

in the House of Representatives on the sorely
vexed Labour Question, there would not be a
happier man in all Colombia than he was. He
was a bitter opponent of the Bill which was being
brought forward, and, being a large employer of
labour, felt that he was entitled to speak with
authority on the subject.

Anstruther and Catalina rode with him to the
city on the day in question and occupied seats in
the gallery of the House. The opposition shown
to her father roused Catalina's wrath to boiling
point, and when the Division was taken and it
was discovered that he was well-nigh unsupported,
she could have shaken her pretty fist in the face
of the very President himself. She left the gallery,
followed by Anstruther, and went down to meet
her father in the vestibule. A small crowd of
journalists and curious folk had collected there,
and for a few moments they were unable to force
a passage through it. Then Don Miguel passed
through the swing doors and looked about him,
as if searching for his daughter and her lover.
In spite of the defeat he had suffered, he carried
himself bravely, looking his enemies in the face
as if he were confident of the justice of his cause.
His appearance was the signal for the commence-
ment of a hostile demonstration. He stopped and
faced his foes, looking at them as a lion might
look at a crowd of yelping curs. Then, before
anyone realised what had happened, there was
the noise of a shot and a loud cry of pain. The
Don staggered, clutched at his breast, and then

fell backwards against the swing doors, whence he slid slowly down to the floor.

With a shout of fury, Anstruther dashed the crowd aside and rushed to his assistance.

But he was too late, Don Miguel D'Araugo was dead !

CHAPTER IV

IF Anstruther lives to be a hundred I am quite
sure that he will not forget the shriek with which
Catalina dashed through the stupefied crowd and
threw herself beside her father's body. For the
time being she was more like a madwoman than
anything else. She placed one arm beneath his
head, and implored him in terms that went to
the heart of everyone present, to speak to her,
to tell her that he was not seriously hurt. Nothing would induce her to believe that he was
dead. Anstruther called one of the bystanders to
his assistance, and between them they carried the
inanimate body to an adjoining room. A doctor
was then sent for, and it was not long before he
put in an appearance. A very brief examination
was sufficient to enable him to give his verdict.
He could do nothing—the worthy old merchant
was beyond the reach of human aid.

On hearing this, Catalina, who was kneeling
beside the couch on which the body had been laid,

turned an agonised face towards them. By this time she must have realised the truth, for, with a little moan that cut Anstruther to the heart, her head fell forward and she collapsed upon the floor in a dead faint.

" Poor girl, poor girl," the doctor muttered, as he lifted her up and placed her in an easy-chair. " She will require a great deal of care, for she has received a terrible shock. If you will let me advise you, Señor, I should take her home with as little delay as possible."

" I will do so," answered the other; " and the body of her father?"

" I will arrange to have it conveyed to Santa Barbara this evening. It will give you time to break the sad intelligence to his wife."

A carriage was soon procured, and Catalina, who had by this time recovered, though she seemed not to know anyone, was placed in it. Compared with their ride into the city that morning, what a miserable return journey it was. The girl sat motionless and silent, staring straight before her, yet apparently seeing nothing. Believing it to be the wisest course, Anstruther did not attempt to disturb her, fearing that if he did she might break down altogether. It seemed an eternity to him before the roofs of Santa Barbara hove in sight. The worst part of the whole miserable business was still to come, for he knew that it would fall to his lot to have to break the news to the widow. He dreaded it more than he could

say. They had been such a devoted couple, that
he dared not think what effect the news would
have upon her. However, it had to be faced, and
it accordingly was. To this day he remembers
that terrible quarter of an hour, and shudders
when he thinks of it.

" Where is Catalina ? " she asked in a calm,
monotonous voice when she had heard everything.

Anstruther replied that she had gone to her
room.

" Then I must go to her. Poor—poor child,
this will break her heart, as it has broken mine."
Even in her own misery she could still think of
others.

When he was alone, the young man walked to
the window and looked out upon the garden. It
seemed impossible to believe that he would never
see that stately figure walking there again or hear
his kindly voice as he paced the winding paths.

That evening Anstruther dined alone, the ladies
preferring to remain shut up together in the solitude of the mother's apartment, where one wept
unceasingly for the husband she had loved so
dearly, and the other sat staring straight before
her as if she were quite unconscious of the tragedy
that had taken place. It was in vain the mother
tried, in spite of her own grief, to comfort her.
She had loved her father with all the strength of
her passionate nature, and to attempt to assuage
her sorrow was, for the time being at least, an
impossibility. She was stunned by the sudden-

ness of the blow, and she made no attempt to rouse herself.

Later in the evening the body of the dead man was brought to Santa Barbara and reverently laid upon a bed in the room which had been prepared for it. The venerable family priest, accompanied by two Sisters, had already arrived. When all the arrangements were complete, one of the latter went to the room where the bereaved women sat in the semi-darkness, and conducted them to the death chamber. Anstruther would have accompanied them, but at the last moment he decided not to do so, feeling that for the present they would prefer to be left alone with their beloved dead. It was not until nearly midnight that he saw Catalina. She came down to bid him " goodnight." Her eyes were heavy, but not with weeping, and she seemed to have aged a dozen years since they had left the house together that morning for Bogotá. She was dressed entirely in black, which had the effect of heightening the pallor of her complexion, to which only her great dark eyes lent relief, and they were full of a sadness such as her lover had never seen in them before.

" Catalina, my poor love," he said, " what can I do or say to comfort you? I would give anything to make you happier. You know that, don't you, dear? "

" I am sure you would," she answered, but it was as if she were talking in her sleep. There

E

was a curious metallic note in her voice that he could not account for. He drew her to him and kissed her passionately, but she was not responsive to his embrace. Her hands and cheeks were as cold as marble.

Seeing that she was quite worn out with grief, Anstruther endeavoured to persuade her to go to bed. At first she refused, but after a time his efforts proved successful, and she consented to lie down if only for a time.

" I shall not sleep," she murmured. " I shall lie awake thinking of him."

Suddenly she seized Anstruther's wrist, and, drawing a little closer, gazed into his face. " Eric," she said, " what has become of the man who killed him? Have they captured him?"

" I am afraid not," was the reply. " He managed to escape during the scene of excitement which followed the committal of the crime."

" But they will be able to find him?" she cried, trembling all over with passion as she spoke. " They must find him. A life for a life. It is the law. He has killed one of the noblest men in the world, and it is but fair that he should pay the penalty of his crime. He *shall*, if I have to kill him myself. You do not think me capable of it! Ah! you do not know me. He has robbed me of the best father that ever a girl had, and I will be revenged."

She drew herself up as she said this, as if she were prepared to carry out her threat there and then.

For the moment her hot Spanish blood was afire, and she looked as if she would have no hesitation at all in carrying out her act of vengeance. Anstruther allowed her to have her say out, hoping that the change from dull torpor to feverish anger might do her good. But he was mistaken. The vehemence which had characterised her a moment before suddenly left her, and she fell back into her former apathetic condition. Seeing this, he led her to the door of her room, where he bade her " good-night." His heart ached for her in her sorrow, and for the reason that he knew he was powerless to help her. Feeling that it would be useless for him to think of retiring to rest himself, he passed into the *patio,* and, seating himself on the edge of the fountain basin, lit a cigar. Overhead the moon was sailing in a cloudless sky, and apart from the splashing of the fountain the only sound to be heard was the cry of a night bird from the hillside across the river. The house was very dark and silent. How different to the previous night, when he and Catalina, happy in their love, had sung and laughed together in the *patio* until the dead man and his wife had been forced to come out and enquire the reason of their merriment. He was musing in this way when the sound of a light footstep on the pavement of the courtyard attracted his attention. A tall, dark figure was approaching him from the shadow of the doorway. It was not, however, until they were standing almost face to face that he discovered the fact that it was his hostess — Donna Mercedes. When last he had seen her she was under the influence of a paroxysm of grief, but now that was all changed, and a strange and almost unnatural calm had descended upon her.

" I have come to thank you," she said, " for your goodness to my poor child. I have just left her."

" I wish that I could have done more," he answered. " I feel so impotent to help in this great time of trouble."

" Ah ! if you did but know what a comfort your presence is to us," she replied, " you would not say that. I don't know what we should have done without you."

She gave him her hand as she said it, and looked up at him in the wan moonlight. There was an almost ghostly look in her face.

" You will be good to her and protect her when I am gone ? " she continued in a voice that was little above a whisper. " Remember, she will have no one but you to turn to then, poor child."

" I will love and protect her with my life," he answered. " But you must not talk like this, Donna Mercedes. To begin with, it would frighten her, and please God, you have happier days in store for you."

But she shook her head.

" No," she answered, " that will never be." Then, drawing a little closer to him, she continued, " Señor Eric, you must not laugh at me when I tell you that my dead husband has warned me to-night that I shall be called upon to follow him within a week. I saw him standing before me as plainly as I can see you now, and that was the message that he gave me. If it were not for Catalina, he could not have brought me better news. With him gone out of it my life has nothing left for me. Now she has found you, and her love will help to compensate her for the loss of her father and myself."

Anstruther began to wonder whether her grief had turned her brain. He had never heard her speak in this way before.

" Nothing can ever compensate her for such a loss," he hastened to say. " You have only to witness her present grief to understand that. Madame, for her sake you must not give way to these thoughts. Consider her, and remember how great is her love for you. The affection she feels for me is of an entirely different nature, and I dare not think what she would do without you. For her sake, be brave."

But again she shook her head.

" I am trying to be brave," she answered, " but a power that is stronger than I has its hand upon me, and, whether I will or will not, is drawing me on along the road that I must travel. And now good-night."

She gave him her hand and then turned and went swiftly away through the shadow into the house, leaving Anstruther more than a little ill

at ease. He remembered his conversation with
the Don, and he now had the opportunity of seeing
what had resulted from it. Even with this example
before him, he could not imagine that the widow
really believed that her natural death was imminent,
nor could he credit her assertion that she had
received a warning from her dead husband to the
effect that she was to follow him. Even making
allowances for inherited superstitions, he could not
conceive any rational being believing such a thing.
But that she did so was only too apparent. For
upwards of an hour he remained in the *patio*,
smoking and endeavouring to come to some understanding of it all. Then giving it up as hopeless,
he threw away what remained of his cigar and made
his way to his room to spend a troubled night.
Again and again the terrible scene in the vestibule
of the Parliament House was enacted for his
benefit. Catalina's shrieks of despair rang continually in his ears. Then the picture would
change to the moonlit *patio* and he would see
Donna Mercedes' white face raised to his in
agonised entreaty and hear her imploring him to
be good to Catalina and to protect her against all
harm when she was gone. Then, strangely
enough, Quintana's evil countenance made its
appearance before him, wearing a diabolical grin
of triumph. He saw him carrying Catalina off
through the almost impenetrable forests. He tried
to follow, but in vain; the interlacing creepers
and the dense underbrush held him prisoner at

every step, twisting and twining themselves about him like the tentacles of an octopus. Just as they were in the act of choking him he woke, with a cold sweat of fear upon his face, to find the light of the new-born day streaming into his room. He rose, bathed, and dressed himself, with the feeling that he had passed through one of the most miserable nights he had ever experienced.

On the day following, Don Miguel was laid to rest, amid the grief of all who had known him. Sad as the event was, Anstruther could not help feeling relieved when the ceremony was over. It had been a heartrending time for everyone concerned, but the effect it produced upon the widow and daughter was as strange as it was sad. The former, after her first outburst of grief, appeared to bear her loss with gentle and almost unnatural resignation; her daughter, on the other hand, raged against Fate and refused to be comforted. She craved for vengeance against the man who had committed the dastardly deed, despite the exhortations of the gentle-spirited priest who had known her from a child, and who tried to wean her from such unchristian thoughts.

" He took my father's life," was her invariable answer to his protests. " He has broken my heart and my mother's. It is only just that he should pay the penalty of his crime."

" But, my daughter," the old man would reply, " it is the act of a christian to forgive.'

" In that case I fear I am no christian," was her answer.

All-absorbing though her desire for revenge might be, however, she was destined to have something else to think about before very long. The funeral had scarcely taken place before a change was noticeable in Donna Mercedes. She made no complaint of feeling ill and yet she seemed to be shrinking away before their very eyes. She no longer felt capable of attending to her household duties, but sat hour after hour, and day after day, looking straight before her as if she were peering in that Unknown Land whither her beloved husband had preceded her, and to which she was to follow him very soon. Do what they might, neither her daughter nor Anstruther could rouse her. The truth was she was literally fading away before their very eyes. All interest in life had departed for her. It was in vain that they sought medical assistance. The doctor declared that it was beyond his power to do anything for her. The rest is soon told. Despite the loving care which had been lavished upon her, she died exactly a fortnight to a day after her husband's assassination, passing peacefully out of life in her sleep, apparently without pain, either physical or mental. It was Catalina who closed her eyes, and then turned her own face, all drawn with pain, to Anstruther. The last blow had fallen—her mother and father were both dead, and, with the exception of her lover, she stood alone in the world. He tried to comfort her, but in vain. Such grief as hers was beyond the reach of human sympathy, however willingly it might be bestowed. As it was, her state of mind positively frightened Anstruther. He began to fear lest her brain might be affected by the trouble she had passed through of late. Then, again, there was the question to be considered as to what her immediate future was to be. He would willingly have thrown conventionality to the winds and have made her his wife there and then, but he had given his solemn promise to the Don that the marriage should not take place for two years, and, under the circumstances, he did not feel justified in breaking it. It was impossible, however, that she should remain where she was, and for many reasons. After the tragedies it had seen of late, Santa Barbara would have exercised too sinister an influence upon her always excitable imagination to be a suitable abiding place for her. Then he remembered what the Don had said to him concerning his own solicitor, Mr. George Tolson. If he could only persuade her to accompany him to England, here was an entirely satisfactory way out of the difficulty. Apart from anything else, the voyage and the change of life and scenery would doubtless prove highly beneficial to her. He determined to write to Mr. Tolson at once and place the matter before him. When the letter was despatched he felt easier in his mind. He told Catalina of what he had done, but she appeared to pay little or no attention to it. Anyone seeing her would scarcely have believed that she was the same girl whose pretty face, winsome ways, and merry laugh had, until lately, been the talk of the countryside. Once more the dismal ceremony was enacted at the graveside, and afterwards Anstruther took Catalina back to Santa Barbara, of which she was now sole mistress. When they had crossed the *patio* and entered the house, the girl left him and went to her room, while Anstruther returned to the *patio* to commune with himself as to what course he should next pursue. He was still turning this over in his mind when a loud knocking was heard on the outer doors. The old manservant, Diaz, hobbled across the pavement, and threw them open, when a horseman, clad in the fashion of the Plains, was seen outside. After a few words with the old man he dismounted and entered the courtyard. Without much interest Anstruther looked at him, only to discover that it was none other than his old enemy, Quintana. What was he doing here? Why had he left San Pedro? He distrusted him both by experience and instinct. Nothing would have induced him to believe that he could do anything for a disinterested motive.

Even with the funeral of Donna Mercedes, Anstruther discovered that his troubles and anxieties were by no means at an end. The strain of the last few weeks had proved too much for the highly wrought girl, and a severe attack of brain fever was the result, and for upwards of a week her reason, if not her life, trembled in the balance. How Anstruther lived through that time he does not know to this day. Every hour was a living nightmare. To add to his misery he was not allowed to see her, for strange to say, his presence had the effect of unduly exciting her. But it was of Quintana that she had the greatest dread. She had not been informed that he was in the house; yet she seemed to be aware of the fact. More than once she believed him to be in her room, and shrieked to those about her to take him away, declaring that he intended to kill her. It was in vain that the doctor and her nurses reasoned with her. Her cry was always the same. In the other portion of the house matters were not progressing any more smoothly. Anstruther resented Quintana's presence in the house, and was at no pains to conceal the fact. The Spaniard, on the other hand, was well aware of the other's feelings towards him, though he, on his side, was too crafty to show it. He had, of course, been made aware of the betrothal, and he was putting his wits to work in every way in order to discover by what manner of means he could not only prevent it, but obtain possession of her for himself. Fifty thousand pounds was a stake worth playing for, and he had set his heart upon winning it. What was more, he wished to be revenged upon the Englishman.

At last Catalina was declared convalescent, and

made her appearance in the world once more—a very ghost of her former self. It was then that she learnt for the first time that Quintana was staying in the house.

"What is he doing here?" she asked of her lover with a flash of her old spirit. "I will not have him here. He frightens me."

"But he can do you no harm, my dearest," answered her lover soothingly. "I am here to protect you."

"But he *will* harm me," she answered, trembling as she spoke. "Keep him away from me. The very look of his face frightens me to death."

To soothe her, Anstruther promised to do what she wished, but he realised the gravity of the task that lay before him. To tell the Spaniard that he must leave the house would only be to bring about a violent rupture which might end in no one knows what. As for Quintana himself, he seemed quite oblivious of the trouble he was causing. He comforted himself with an airy grace and a charm of manner that with many women would have proved irresistible. He anticipated Catalina's every want, and when she was present, treated Anstruther with a condescension that drove the other nearly beside himself with rage. Why he did not return to the ranch Anstruther could not understand, though he hazarded a very good guess. One day, in a fit of exasperation, he hinted that he should do so, but the suggestion was received with such an explosion of temper that he did not venture upon it again.

After her first outburst against him, Catalina appeared to take little or no notice of the Spaniard. Then, to her lover's amazement, she seemed somewhat to relax her feeling of dislike for him. It was as if he had hypnotised her into taking him into favour. As for her behaviour towards Anstruther, it might have almost been described as cold. While he knew that she was not as yet properly responsible for her actions, he was none the less deeply hurt by this treatment. He was too proud, however, to speak to her upon the subject. But this did not prevent him from hating the Spaniard as he had never thought it possible for him to hate anybody. It would have needed only a small spark to have brought about an explosion. But Quintana's triumph was destined to be short-lived. One day it was necessary for Anstruther to visit the capital on business. He returned just as dusk was falling. He gave up his horse and entered the house. If the truth must be told, he was in a very despondent frame of mind. The time was drawing near for him to take Catalina away from Colombia, if he were going to take her at all. But what about Quintana? That he had an uncanny influence over her was quite certain; would he use it to prevent her leaving the country? He made his way to the room which had been the favourite apartment of Catalina's mother. As he reached the door he paused, for the sound of a voice reached him from within. He recognised it as Quintana's. But there was something in it that he had never noticed before.

"You cannot escape me," he was saying. "You are mine, body and soul. To-morrow night you will leave this place with me, and I warn you that, if you let fall as much as a hint, his life will pay the penalty."

Fearing lest Quintana might come out of the room, Anstruther turned on his heel and went back to the *patio*, where he seated himself on the fountain edge and tried to think what was best to be done. There could be no doubt that the Spaniard must be outwitted, if he wished to save Catalina, and the only way to do that was to get her to the sea and on board the mail boat *en route* for England with as little delay as possible. It would be a dangerous business, but he could not afford to think of that. Her reason, perhaps her very life, depended on the promptness of his action. He determined to commence operations immediately. He was still turning this over in his mind when Quintana entered the *patio*. There was a look of triumph upon his face which he was unable to conceal. He passed Anstruther without a word, and went out through the gates.

"I wonder what mischief he is about now?" said the other to himself. But as he was unable to answer the question to his own satisfaction, he put it aside and went into the house in search of Catalina. He found her seated in the room in which he had heard the Spaniard talking to her. She was crouched upon a settee near the window, in an attitude betokening the deepest dejection.

Anstruther crossed and seated himself beside her.

"Catalina," he said, "I can see that you are unhappy. Will you not confide in me and tell me what I can do. It cuts me to the heart to see you like this."

As he said this he placed his hand upon her shoulder as if to draw her to him, but she shrank away as if in terror. There was a look in her eyes like that of a rabbit fascinated by a snake.

"You can do nothing," she whispered. "Leave me to my fate, or I shall drag you down into the pit into which I am falling myself."

"Hush, hush, my love," he said soothingly. "You must not talk like that. Leave everything to me, and I will take care that no harm befalls you. Will you be brave, Catalina, and do exactly as I ask you without questioning the why and wherefore?"

"I have no bravery left," she answered. "You do not know the power he has over me. When he looks at me as he does, I have no will of my own, my brain becomes numbed, and I am forced to do his bidding."

Anstruther cursed the Spaniard under his breath, but aloud he said:

"That is only your fancy. The fellow has not as much power over you as I have, and I swear to you upon my honour that no evil shall befall you while you love me. You do love me still, Catalina?"

"I love you as fondly as ever," she replied.

" But what is the use of that when he will not allow me to become your wife ? "

" Won't he," said the other vindictively. " We'll see about that. I don't want to boast, but I am as good a man as Señor Bartolomé Quintana any day of the week, and I am quite prepared to let him know it."

" No, no," she cried passionately, " you must not run any risks. You do not know him as I do." Then sinking her voice to a whisper, she added, with an impressiveness that was not lost upon her companion, " He is the Devil in human shape. We are powerless to fight against him."

" But we are going to fight against him. Your father gave you to me, and I am not going to be cheated out of my prize by any Spaniard that ever walked the earth, however great a villain he may be."

But she only shook her head wearily, and Anstruther realised that, far from being consoled by what he had said to her, she was more convinced than ever that Quintana was stronger than he. To continue the argument, he told himself, would be worse than useless in her present state of mind. It was more than ever borne in upon him that he would have to act upon his own initiative without relying upon her in any way. But would he be able to get her away from Santa Barbara and Bogotá without Quintana being aware of the fact ?

At any rate, he was going to do his best. Then inspiration came to him. He remembered Diaz, the Don's faithful old major-domo, who loved Catalina as truly as if she were his own daughter, and who hated the Spaniard as much as he did himself. "If anyone can help me," he said to himself, "Diaz is that man."

He set off in search of him.

CHAPTER V

BY making enquiries, Anstruther eventually
located Diaz on a bench beside the river, a
favourite spot of his, where he was smoking his
cigarette, and doubtless pondering over the sad
events of the last few weeks. He was a queer-
looking little fellow, some sixty-five years of age,
the greater part of which he had spent in Don
Miguel's service. He was possessor of a quaint
little nut-cracker face, wrinkled like a crab apple.
His devotion to the family he had served so long
was proverbial, and woe betide the person who
should have the temerity to say anything in dis-
paragement of anyone connected with it. As a
rule he was not partial to Englishmen, but he
had liked Anstruther from the first—a fact for
which that gentleman had reason to be thankful
in this time of great anxiety. He was going to
pin all his chance of happiness on the old fellow's
honesty, with the full assurance that it would not
be misplaced. Should he betray him, then he
would be lost indeed. The old man on seeing him,

rose and bowed. It was evident that he was somewhat surprised at seeing him in such a place, though he was too courteous to say so.

"I have come in search of you, Diaz," said the other, "for, if you will allow me, I should like to have a serious conversation with you."

"I am at your Excellency's service now, as always," replied the old man.

Anstruther seated himself on the bench and offered his companion a cigarette, which he accepted with the air of a Castillian Grandee.

"Diaz," said the other, "you have faithfully served the D'Araugo family for a great number of years, and I have the best of reasons for knowing that you would not like the Señorita Catalina to be made more unhappy than she is at present."

"Indeed, no, Señor," he answered. "I swear by the Holy Saints that I would give what remains of my useless old life if only I could see her as happy as she once was. But that, alas, I fear will never be. Poor maid, she has indeed passed through sad times. What can I do, Señor? You have but to tell me, and you may rely upon my performing it if it is in my power to do so."

Anstruther rose from his seat and looked carefully around him before he replied, for he wanted to make quite sure that Quintana was not in the vicinity. When he had convinced himself on this point he re-seated himself, motioning to Diaz to follow his example. For some moments he paused, not knowing how to enter upon what he had to say. Then he moved a little nearer Diaz, and speaking in a low voice, said, " I am right, I believe, in supposing that you are not particularly attracted by Señor Quintana?"

The old man's reply was emphatic, if it was nothing else.

" I hate him," he growled, " and you, Señor, should hate him much more, for he is trying his best to steal my young mistress from you."

" I know it," was Anstruther's reply, " and that is my reason for coming to you to-night. Diaz, something must be done, or her life will be ruined. He has cast a spell over her, and she is so frightened of him that she is falling completely into his power."

He went on to describe the interview he had just had with her and the reception it met with. The old man heard him in silence, but Anstruther saw from his face that not a syllable escaped him.

" And what do you intend to do, Señor?" asked the latter, when the younger man had finished. " Something ought to be attempted at once. That man is capable of anything. He would think no more of murdering her or you than he would of eating his dinner. He would have been turned out of this house long since had my dear master been still alive; or, better still, he would never have been allowed to enter it after the way he behaved the last time he was here. Have you any scheme in your mind, Señor?"

" I have," answered Anstruther, " and it is

concerning him that I have come to you to-night."

He then went on to tell the other of his plan to take Catalina to England with him, in accordance with the old Don's express wishes.

" As matters stand now," he said in conclusion, " it is quite certain that she must go at once—but how is it to be done? If Quintana suspects anything, he will stick at nothing to prevent our departure."

" But he must not become aware of it. You must fly without his knowledge."

" It is very easy to talk about flying," Anstruther retorted, " but how is it to be accomplished? He watches me as a cat does a mouse, and now that he must surely know that I am in the secret of his villainy he will be even more cunning than before. He would not hesitate a second at shooting me if he caught me taking the Señorita away from him, and for her sake, as well as my own, I do not want that to happen. However, got away she must be and, as you say, at once. It would be impossible for us to leave in the day-time; consequently the attempt must be made at night."

" And whither would you go? Would you make your way to Honda and thence to the coast, or proceed through the State of Bolivar to Magdalena ? "

" Through Bolivar, by all means, but to Cartagena instead of Magdalena. There, if we are lucky, we shall just be in time to pick up the steamer for England. I shall not know a moment's peace until I am on board and the voyage has begun."

"In the meantime," said the old man slowly, "what I have to do is to find you the means of reaching the port. It is a great distance, and through terrible country. You will want men who can be trusted to go with you. I will find them — also a sufficient number of sure-footed mules to carry yourselves and your baggage. I know of two men who can be trusted implicitly. They are Dominique and Numez, the sons of old Jiminez Menzebel. They owe all they have in the world to the goodness of my late master. They would serve his daughter and yourself to the death. What is more, they hate Quintana from the bottom of their hearts."

"They would probably be able to find the necessary mules for us," said Anstruther. "When do you think you could see them?"

"I will do so to-night," the old man replied. "When it is quite dark I will go to their house and lay the matter before them."

"Tell them I will reward them liberally," Anstruther continued. "Do not let the question of money be considered at all. Though you may not know it, I am a rich man, and I am prepared to venture anything to get my darling out of that villain's clutches."

"Ah! Señor," said the old man, "I cannot pay you a greater compliment than to say that you are worthy to be her husband. I have known and loved her since the day of her birth. It was

I who taught her to walk — who led her first pony, and who has watched her grow into her gracious womanhood—and to think that it should all end like this. Father and mother both dead, and she compelled to fly from her home like a thief in the night."

Tears rolled down the worthy old man's furrowed cheeks.

" You must not take it so much to heart, Diaz,'' said Anstruther soothingly. " You will see your young mistress again, please God, and in happier days."

But he only shook his head.

" No," he answered, " I must not count on that. I have well-nigh reached the length of my days, and when I bid her ' farewell ' to-morrow night, something tells me that it will be for ever. Now, it would be better that we should return to the house, but it must be by different ways, lest that monster in human shape should see us and become suspicious. It is just as well for him that he did not live fifty years ago. If he had he would probably find that his supper to-night would not be likely to agree with him."

With this sinister suggestion the old man hobbled off and was presently lost to sight among the trees on the right of the estate. Anstruther, on the other hand, remained where he was for upwards of ten minutes, when he too set off for the house by the way he had come. The old man's assurance that he could arrange everything for their flight had raised his drooping spirits, and perhaps for this reason he felt better disposed towards the world in general, always excepting Quintana, than he had done since the assassination of Don Miguel. The only thing that weighed upon him was the period that must necessarily elapse before they could put their scheme into execution. During that time he must devote all his energies to keeping Quintana from suspecting anything. For this reason he determined not to say anything on the subject to Catalina, fearing lest the Spaniard might force her to reveal it to him.

If that should happen he knew he might as well resign all hope of ever making her his wife.

When he reached the house he discovered that Catalina had been persuaded by the old house-keeper to go to bed, and, in consequence, he and Quintana supped alone together. It was by no means a cheerful meal; although Anstruther did his best to appear at ease, he made but a feeble success of it. The Spaniard, on the other hand, made no attempt to conceal his ill humour; he helped himself repeatedly to the bottle of *aguardiente*, and as its contents waned his insolence increased. The Englishman found that it took him all his time to control his temper. The scarcely veiled insults which were directed at him made him feel as if he could be at the other's throat. Had it not been for the warning glances which were cast at him by old Diaz, who waited upon them, there is no knowing what might have happened. But to his credit, be it said, he managed to keep his temper, and when they rose from the table he was able to congratulate himself on having come through the ordeal so satisfactorily. Leaving the other to finish his bottle, he made his way to the *patio* in the hope of obtaining an interview with the old manservant, nor was he disappointed. He had not been there many minutes before he heard the sound of a shuffling footstep on the pavement, and Diaz made his appearance. The old man was in a state of great excitement.

" I have just looked in at him," he said, "and found him asleep. But we must not be long, for I do not know how soon he will wake. Curse the dog ! I wish he might never open his eyes again. Caramba ! He thinks he is going to be master here, but he is mistaken. He will sing a different tune ere long. Now listen, Señor. I have seen Nuñez and Dominique, and they have agreed to go with you to the coast. They are faithful, as well as brave, and, what is more, they have good reason to hate Quintana as much as I do."

" But what about mules ? " asked Anstruther. " Have you been able to procure them ? "

" They are to obtain ten for me to-night," was the answer. " They will purchase them in their own name in order that suspicion may not be aroused. At midnight to-morrow night they will have them in waiting in the palm grove near the crossing a mile or so from here."

" That is good news," said Anstruther, as he shook the other heartily by the hand. " Whatever success attends our enterprise we shall owe to you. Please God, I may be able to make it up to you some day."

"Make the Señorita happy, Señor, that is all I ask of you. You have said nothing to her, I suppose, on the subject of your flight?"

"I have not even seen her," was the reply. "She had retired to her room before I returned to the house. No, I shall not say anything to her at all about it until the time arrives for action. That will be quite soon enough. But how are we to make sure that Quintana will be in bed by midnight? Sometimes he remains up until the early hours of the morning."

"Leave that to me, Señor," said Diaz, with a chuckle. "I will take good care that he gives no trouble. To-morrow old Maria, who, as you know is to be trusted implicitly, shall pack such things as may be necessary for my young mistress to take away with her, and, as soon as it is dark, they shall leave the house for the rendezvous. You see, I have thought of everything. Even to the matter of the provisions which it will be necessary for you to take with you on the journey."

"You are thoughtfulness itself, my dear Diaz," answered Anstruther, "and if the dear old Don can see what is going on, he must be as grateful to you as I am. But what is that?"

The sound of a heavy footfall had arrested his attention: it was the step of one who walked with an uncertain tread, and both of them were easily able to guess to whom it belonged.

"I must go," whispered Diaz. "It would never do for him to find me here. He is the worse for the liquor he has taken, so do not let him draw you into a quarrel. He would think as little of thrusting a knife into you as I should do of carving a chicken. Make an excuse, Señor, and retire to your room as soon as possible."

"You can trust me, Diaz," Anstruther replied. "Hot tempered as I am, he will find me one of the most peaceable men alive to-night."

"The Saints be thanked for that," he heard the old man mutter as he turned and left him.

He had barely disappeared into the shadow before Quintana reeled into the *patio*.

One glance was sufficient to show Anstruther that he was as intoxicated as the proverbial fiddler. Anstruther had seen him like this more than once before, and he therefore knew what he had to expect.

"And you call yourself a good comrade," the other began. "*Demonios!* I'd rather have the poorest *Llanero* for company than you. You won't drink, you won't sing, you won't do anything. Perhaps it's because I am not good enough for your English Mighty Highness." As he said this he staggered and came within an ace of falling into the fountain pond. His attitude, as he recovered himself, was so absurd that, before he knew what he was doing, Anstruther was foolhardy enough to indulge in a laugh. In a second the Spaniard's fiery blood was ablaze. Dragging a revolver from his pocket, he pointed it and pulled the trigger. Drunk though he was, his aim was almost too accurate, for the bullet whizzed close past Anstruther's right ear and bedded itself in the oak doorway behind him. This was carrying matters too far, he argued, and immediately closed with his assailant. The struggle that ensued was but a short one. With his left he caught the wrist of the hand that held the revolver, while with his right he dealt his enemy a blow upon the left temple that sent him down to measure his length upon the pavement.

"Good Heavens, I hope I have not killed him," cried Anstruther, as he saw that the other lay just as he had fallen and without making any attempt to rise. "Confound that silly laugh of mine. If I hadn't done it it is possible we might have managed to separate without a quarrel. If he is not dead he will hate me all the more for this."

He knelt down beside the Spaniard and examined him carefully. The man was not dead, only stunned. The drink he had consumed was possibly as much accountable for this as the blow he had received. While he was examining him, Diaz ran back into the *patio*, crying, "What has happened? What has happened?"

"Nothing very much," Anstruther replied coolly. "He did his best to shoot me and I knocked him down, that is all."

"Is he dead?"

"Not a bit of it. He will live to do a lot more mischief yet. But it is a wonderful thing that he did not put an end to my career. The bullet whizzed past my ear, and, if I am not mistaken, you will find it in the oak door yonder. I think while I am about it I will take possession of his revolver in order to avoid future trouble.''

" But what are we to do with him ? " asked the old man, who was trembling violently. " He cannot be allowed to remain here.''

" Then let us take him up between us and carry him to bed. He will be all right when he has slept off the effects of his carouse. For some reason I am inclined to be sorry that I did not hit him a little harder. It would have rid the world of one of the most consummate scoundrels that ever walked upon it.''

Between them they picked up the inanimate body and carried it to his own apartment, where they laid it upon the bed. A large bruise was beginning to show on the left side of the forehead, and there was every possibility of it assuming larger proportions as time progressed. Having removed his boots and loosened his collar, the others left him and sought their respective apartments, not, however, without a lament on the elder's part that events should have turned out in such an untoward manner.

Next morning neither Catalina nor Quintana made their appearance at breakfast, or the meal which, in Spanish households, is equivalent to that repast. The former preferred to take it in her own apartment, while the latter, so Diaz declared, was either too unwell or too sulky to leave his room.

"You must have struck him with great force, Señor," remarked the latter with evident delight, "for he has a bruise the size of a turkey's egg, which is fast turning purple. Let him remain in his room as long as he pleases. It will be the better for us if he stays there altogether. I, for one, shall certainly not be sorry."

But, as it appeared, their amiable desire was not destined to be realised, for shortly after mid-day the gentleman in question made his appearance, and, much to Anstruther's surprise, endeavoured to behave as if nothing out of the common had occurred. He made no allusion to the events of the previous night, but once, when he thought he was not being watched, Anstruther detected an expression upon his face that showed him that he was not so forgetful as he evidently desired that other people should think. If ever there was murder written upon a human countenance, it was inscribed on his. As for the loss of his revolver, he never for one moment alluded to it. Having fortified himself with a couple of glasses of *aguardiente*, he lit a cigar and left the house, making his way in the direction of the stables. News reached the house later that he had helped to console himself by thrashing one of the grooms who had had the temerity to smile on observing the bruise with which his forehead was ornamented. The result was that he came within an ace of being mobbed by the victim's companions who, during the Don's lifetime, had not been accustomed to such treatment, and told him so. In consequence,

he returned to the *hacienda* in a still more un-
amiable frame of mind than he had left it. While
he had been absent Anstruther had managed to
obtain an interview with the Señorita, whom he
found still in the same depressed condition as when
he had last seen her. Her only interest seemed
to be her fear of Quintana. The man haunted her
like a nightmare, and at every uncommon sound
she quailed as if she feared he were coming to
molest her. It was in vain that Anstruther argued
with her and endeavoured to convince her that she
had nothing to fear from the fellow; he tried to
make her see that she had good and staunch
friends about her who, if necessity should arise,
would protect her even with their lives. She refused, however, to be comforted. Her latest belief
was that he had stolen her soul from her, and that
she would never know peace or happiness again.
It was indeed a pitiable state of mind for so young
and beautiful a girl. But, Anstruther argued continually, if he could but get her away out of the
country and far distant from her present surroundings, she would soon regain her strength and
throw off the black cloud which had descended
and enveloped her. If he had loved her truly
before he loved her a thousand times more now
in this terrible time of mental distress. Few
people would have recognised in this sober and
staid young man, fighting for the reason and life
of the woman he loved, the happy-go-lucky young
undergraduate whose follies had angered his father
so much and had led to the exile from the home to
which he was about to return as master.

So does love, combined with anxiety, work a
change in even the most reckless and volatile
character.

Later on in the day Diaz informed him that
Catalina's baggage had been packed and was ready
to be sent to the rendezvous in the palm grove
near the crossing. So far the young lady herself
was quite unaware of the plans that were being
mapped out for her rescue. The news, they had
agreed, was not to be broken to her until a few
moments before it would be necessary for them to
start. To do so sooner would be to run the risk
of Quintana's finding out what was about to
happen, which would be the reverse of satisfactory
for all parties concerned. At her request Maria,
the old housekeeper, had for the past few nights
slept in her room, and it was arranged that she
should wake her, if she should be asleep, at the
appointed time. Once dressed, she was to make
her way as quietly as possible to the *patio*, where
her lover and old Diaz would be awaiting her
coming. After that they were to cover the mile
and a half that separated them from the palm
grove at as fast a speed as possible. Once there,
Anstruther repeatedly informed himself, the rest
would be merely a matter of flight. At supper
that evening it soon became evident that Quintana
had by no means recovered his equanimity.
Whether it was the scene at the stables, the fact
that he had not seen Catalina all day, or the sight
of his enemy seated opposite, that was to be held
accountable for it, I cannot say. It is sufficient,

however, to put it on record that he ate but little, and cursed his luck, his surroundings, and his probable future with a fluency that did credit to his cosmopolitan upbringing. Anstruther listened to him in silence, but with disgust written on every line of his face. He thanked his stars that after that night he would be rid of him for ever, the more especially as the fact was self evident that, if he continued in the lines he was now pursuing, he would be ripe for any devilry before the next few days should pass over his head. By the time they rose from the table he was in a maudlin condition; only a few more glasses would be required to render him hopelessly intoxicated, and these few he was evidently quite prepared to partake of. Leaving him to his own company, Anstruther made his way to his own bedroom, to put together the few things he intended to take with him. His money he stowed away round his waist in a belt, retaining sufficient to re-imburse Diaz for the mules and various expenses to which he had been put. He did not intend to change his attire until the last moment, and for obvious reasons. Drunk though he was, Quintana might still have sufficient wit left to draw his own conclusions from such a proceeding. For this reason he remained just as he had dined. He soon had cause to be thankful that he had done so, for he had not been smoking long in the *patio* before his enemy made his appearance, with Catalina's guitar suspended from his shoulders. His mood had changed from the bucolic to the musical, and,

G

seating himself in a vacant chair beside Anstruther, he struck a few incoherent chords. Then he burst into song. Never did a man make a more pitiable exhibition of himself. Presumably his effort was a love-song, but it would have required much discernment to have satisfactorily settled the point.

"You don't sing, Señor Anstruther," he grumbled at last. "Let me tell you that you have not the gift of making yourself agreeable to others. You are as unsympathetic as your own dismal island."

In reply, though his gorge was rising against the other, Anstruther endeavoured to say something conciliatory. It was wasted, however, for Quintana was struggling hopelessly with the introduction to the famous Toreador Song from "Carmen." Having found that impossible, he managed to get on to his feet and staggered back into the house in search of more refreshment. As he did so the French clock in the dead woman's boudoir chimed the hour of eleven. As he heard it a thrill ran through Anstruther and set his heart beating wildly. In half an hour, if all went well, it would be time for them to start. Then farewell to Santa Barbara, its joys and its sorrows, and hey for the great world across the sea. He was thinking that it behoved him to repair to his room in order to change his clothes, when Diaz made his appearance from the house and tiptoed softly towards him.

"He is safe," he whispered. "I drugged his liquor, and now he will give no trouble, at least not for several hours to come. Hurry, Señor, for however confident we may be it behoves us not to neglect an opportunity.''

'' And the Señorita ? ''

'' I have told her, and old Maria is assisting her to dress even now.''

Anstruther did not wait to hear more, but hastened with all dispatch to his room, whence he once more emerged in the picturesque costume of a ranchman of the plains. He returned to the *patio*, where Diaz was anxiously awaiting his coming. So far there was no sign of Catalina or the old woman, a circumstance which gave them cause for no little anxiety.

'' What can have happened to detain her ? '' was the question they asked each other.

Just, however, as Diaz was thinking it behoved him to go in search of her, she made her appearance, dressed in a riding costume, but apparently unconscious of what was required of her. Anstruther took her in his arms, and kissed her tenderly, and then having bade old Maria *adieu*, and led by Diaz, they passed through the familiar gate and out into the still night beyond. On the crest of the slight eminence by which the river ran, and on which Catalina had pulled up her horse to bid him farewell on the day on which he had set out for San Pedro, they turned and looked their last at the little collection of buildings in the valley below. Would they ever see them again ? That was a question that only the future could answer.

In something under half an hour they had reached the palm grove, where they found Nunez and Dominique anxiously awaiting their coming. Over their farewell to the faithful old servant who had done so much for them both, and whose grief at parting with him was heartbreaking to witness, I must draw a veil. Let it suffice that ere the clocks had struck the half-hour after midnight they were well on their way.

Of that long and wearisome journey, its trials, its difficulties, and its dangers, it is not my intention to say very much. For a variety of reasons it was impossible for them to travel very fast. They had a delicately nurtured girl with them, and her presence alone was sufficient to prevent their pushing forward as quickly as they would otherwise have done. During the whole of the time she was haunted by a fear that Quintana would overtake them, and that she would once more fall into his clutches. Anstruther's heart ached for her, but he felt himself powerless to do more than he was already doing to help her. At night, in the silence of the forest, she would shriek from the shelter they had improvised for her that the Spaniard was at hand, that he was only waiting for his opportunity to seize her. Such a hold had he obtained upon her that she could think of nothing else. Bodily fatigue was unknown to her. She could ride from early morn till dewy eve without the faintest sign of being tired, until the other members of the party began to feel that they were mere babes so far as endurance was concerned.

At last, and none too soon, they came within a measurable distance of their destination, and two days later clattered over the bridges which connected the island of Cartagena with the mainland. Their long journey was at an end, and, provided that Quintana was not there to receive them, which was hardly likely, it might be said to have been successfully accomplished. The steamer by which they were to sail was expected on the day following. In the meantime, Anstruther installed himself and his charge at the principal hotel in the quaint little town, which had been sacked by Drake in 1585, and had repulsed Vernon in 1741. As a token of his gratitude to the two faithful fellows who had accompanied him, he handed a considerable sum of money, at the same time making them a present of the mules and their equipment. It was with mutual regret and the heartiest of good wishes that they parted company.

" Farewell Señor and the most noble Señorita," said they. " May your lives know no shadow, and may sorrow never darken your door."

Early next morning, and well up to her schedule time, the steamer made her appearance and anchored in the harbour. Catalina and Anstruther, who, with a snuffy old priest, were the only passengers from Cartagena, hastened to board her. The cargo was quickly stowed, and by mid-day the vessel was on her way once more —bound for Blewfields *en route* for Jamaica, where they were to transfer themselves and their baggage to another and larger steamer for England.

" Catalina, my darling," whispered Anstruther,

as they leaned upon the rail and watched the dwindling coast line, "can you believe that you are safe, and that your troubles are at an end?"

She pressed his hand lovingly in answer. But was she safe after all?

END OF PART I

PART II

CHAPTER VI

THE great Miss Pinnifer, most renowned of all schoolmistresses, sat in her *sanctum sanctorum,* as she delighted to call it, one wet day in October, between the hours of eleven and twelve in the forenoon. She studied a letter she held in her hand, and which she had already perused three times. To judge, however, from the expression on her face, she was still as far from comprehending its meaning as when she had first read it. For Miss Pinnifer to be at a loss to understand anything is scarcely conceivable; her governesses and her young ladies would have scouted the idea, had you said as much to them. Miss Pinnifer nonplussed !—why, she would have routed all the learned professors at the rival Universities with the greatest ease had occasion demanded such a thing. Even the Vicar of the parish, the Reverend Aloysius McFadden, walked humbly before her, while, as for the curates—they, poor wretches, absolutely grovelled at her feet. Was she not the sole proprietress of the famous Seminary for

Young Ladies—that terribly expensive finishing school which is known as Athena House, and is situated in that most fashionable quarter of all Brighton, namely, Senlac Square? Let me tell you, that to have it known that you were one of Miss Pinnifer's young ladies was almost akin to being of the Blood Royal. In some instances I have heard that it counted for more—much more. All told, there were twenty of these charming young ladies on the boarding list, the very plainest of which—if there happened to be a plain one, which I very much doubt—was lovely enough to set the heart of Impressionable Man beating like a thermantidote paddle. To put the finishing touches to the education of these *houris* there were four governesses, and to help the governesses five professors, not, of course, including the Vicar, who conducted a Scripture class on Thursday afternoons at half-past three, and was so nervous, poor man, that he scarcely knew how to hold his book; and on one occasion made the memorable mistake of declaring that it was the whale that sat under the gourd and fed Jonah in the wilderness, much to the horror of Miss Pinnifer, and, as you may suppose, to the amusement of the younger and more frivolous members of his audience.

Athena House itself is a tall and stately building, dating back to the Georgian period, and had culture written on every stone of it, from the elegant pillars of the portico to the moulding that decorated the face of the wall below the eaves. Even the knocker on the front door was of classic design, representing as it did Athena's head. Broad brass rods upheld the dainty short blinds of the bedroom windows, the snowiest of curtains supported them on either side, while even the class-rooms, which looked out upon the square, were not like such apartments in other and less expensive scholastic establishments. The furniture in the various rooms was handsome, if not luxurious. It was for these things, as much as for the curriculum, that the parents paid so heavily, and you may be quite sure that Miss Pinnifer found the advertisement an excellent one in every sense of the word. As she was wont to remark to anxious mothers when they called upon her to arrange for dear Ethelberta's finishing—" My dear madame, it has always been my most earnest endeavour to make my establishment represent the homes of dear pupils as far as possible. A lifelong experience of scholastic work has led me to the conclusion that her surroundings, if by such a term one may so express it, play a most important part in the formation of a young lady's character." The mother, though perhaps scarcely understanding the drift of the assertion, would, of course, hasten to agree with her, and Miss Ethelberta de Brown-Jones from that moment would be entrusted without misgiving to the tender care of that most wonderful lady, Miss Eleanor Pinnifer, of Athena House, Senlac Square, Brighton.

I have already said that Miss Pinnifer had thrice read the letter she held in her hand. She now perused it a fourth time. There was certainly a puzzled expression on her face as she laid it on her writing-table and sat for a few minutes gazing out of the window into the square, where the rain was beating pitilessly down upon the leafless trees.

"It really is an extraordinary communication," she said to herself. "I confess that I am quite at a loss to understand it. Indeed, I cannot say that in all my experience I remember having received such another. I must see Tibbits, and hear what she thinks of it."

She rose and rang the bell. When it was answered by a neat maidservant, she bade the latter carry "Miss Pinnifer's compliments to Miss Tibbits, and ask that lady if she would be obliging enough to wait upon Miss Pinnifer as soon as she could make it convenient."

Miss Tibbits hastened to obey, partly out of curiosity to discover what she was summoned for, but more, perhaps, because she was aware that her employer was a lady of somewhat uncertain temper, who had a firmly rooted objection to being kept waiting. Punctuality with Miss Pinnifer was not a principle; it amounted almost to a mania. It was a commonplace in the square that you could set your clocks by what went on in Athena House. The young ladies' rising bell sounded at half-past six to the tick, the breakfast bell at eight, the school bell at nine, the luncheon bell at one, and so on throughout the day. Terrible indeed was the lot of the teacher, the pupil or the maid, who was so much as a minute behind time. *" Ein wenig zu spät ist viel zu spät "* was her motto, and she acted up to it.

When Miss Tibbits entered the *sanctum sanctorum* of her omnipotent mistress it was to find that lady pacing up and down the room, her hands clasped behind her back, and an air of mystery pervading her whole being. Her grey hair, with the old-fashioned corkscrew curls on either side of her forehead, to say nothing of the cap which sat upon her head like a Roman helmet, gave her an air of dignity seldom seen in these unregenerate days.

On hearing the door close she turned and faced her subordinate.

" Tibbits," she began, " we have now been associated for upwards of twenty years." Here she picked up the letter from the writing-table. " I place great reliance, as I think you are aware, upon your judgment. Be good enough, therefore, to peruse this document and give me your opinion upon it. For my own part, I must confess that I scarcely know what construction to place upon it."

As she spoke she handed the letter to Miss Tibbits, who took it with the air of one who has had the execution of an important commission confided to her, and who is determined to prove worthy of the trust at any cost to herself. Miss Tibbits is a lady who would have inspired confidence in the redoubtable Fouché himself. She was a spinster of between fifty and fifty-five years of age, tall, angular, and extraordinarily thin. Like her employer, she invariably dressed in black, wore a cap with black ribbons, and sported a pair of corkscrew curls, which, if they did not quite equal Miss Pinnifer's in size and silkiness of texture, more than surpassed them in rigidity.. She united the duties of housekeeper, matron, duenna, and private secretary, administered physic to the young ladies when physic was required, and generally acted as her employer's trusted factotum. Needless to say, she was cordially detested by everyone save the actual head of the establishment. So much for Miss Tibbits.

The lady I have just described read the letter carefully and then re-read it. She had picked up her cue, and was prepared to agree that it certainly was an extraordinary document, the more so as it had come to Athena House of all places in the world. She cudgelled her brains in the hope of being able to find its parallel, but without success.

" Well, Tibbits, what do you think of it ? " asked Miss Pinnifer, when the other had replaced the sheet of writing-paper on the table. " Is it not as I observed to you a few minutes since, an extraordinary document ? "

" It certainly is peculiar," replied the lady she addressed. For once in her life it seemed to her that she stood on the edge of a mystery. " It is a most singular communication. May I ask if you have any knowledge of the writer ? "

" None whatever," answered her employer,

"save that I have looked into the London Post
Office Directory and I have satisfied myself that
there is such a firm of solicitors as 'Tolson,
Matthews, and Durnford,' and that its offices are
in Lincoln's Inn Fields. Otherwise I am as much
in the dark as you are. Be so good, my dear
Tibbits, as to read the letter aloud to me once
more."

Miss Tibbits again took up the sheet of writing-
paper, and having given a nervous cough, according to custom, commenced to read. The letter,
it appeared, was dated from the office of the firm
mentioned above, and was signed by the senior
partner, Mr. George Bramwell Tolson. It ran as
follows :—

MY DEAR MADAME,
        In the list of scholastic establishments of
the highest grade it has been pointed out to me
that not one has attained the eminence of Miss
Pinnifer's Seminary for Young Ladies, situated
in Senlac Square, Brighton. In saying this I
am paying you no idle compliment, for I might
say that I have been occupied during the last
fortnight, searching high and low, for such an
establishment as I now have the pleasure of
knowing yours to be. With your permission,
therefore, I will, without further preamble,
place both my wants and my position before you
and leave you to judge of their respective merits.

As you will surmise from the printed heading
of this letter, I am a member of a well-known

firm of London solicitors. There are times, as doubtless you will readily understand, when we find ourselves called upon, by the exigences of our profession, to undertake tasks which, not to put too fine a point upon it, are, to say the least, curious. This must certainly be accounted one of them.

At the risk of trespassing on your time, and also upon your good nature, I will endeavour to explain my meaning. The case I put before you is a singular one, and for several reasons: to a student of human nature—such as yourself —it will, I am sure, be one of absorbing interest. Short as the history is, I venture to believe that it will not be without its interesting side. Judge, my dear madame, for yourself.

Many years ago I was somewhat more of a traveller than most Englishmen aspire to be— even in these tourist days. Europe I know by heart, India and the Far East I have visited once, Australia and South Africa twice. My favourite hunting ground, however, is South America, to which I have paid repeated visits. Now, it so happened that while on my first visit to Venezuela and Colombia I made the acquaintance, while in the little-known city of Bogotá, capital of the latter State, of a certain wealthy merchant, Don Miguel D'Araugo by name. He possessed a charming wife, and a daughter who was then about ten years of age. His country estate was a remarkably beautiful one, and was situated a few miles from the city. There he

entertained me on repeated occasions, and I may
say that each one found me adding to the respect
I already felt for him.   He was a man for whom
it would be impossible to entertain anything but
a feeling of admiration—he was so honest, so
charitable, so sincere in all his undertakings.
The last time that I saw him he told me of a
strange presentiment that he had, which was to
the effect that, however much we might try, we
should never meet again.   I did my best to
reason with him; I tried to make him see that
this was merely a superstition on his part, and
one that Time would surely dispel.   But it was
of no use, I could not argue him out of it—do
what I would.   To say that I was amazed at
his weakness would not at all express my feelings, for I knew by experience that he was a
hard-headed man of business, and consequently
one of the least likely to allow such morbid
thoughts to take possession of him.   Imagine
my feelings, therefore, when I discovered that
his amiable wife also shared them!   She, also,
was firmly convinced that we should never meet
again.   I can assure you that I left the city of
Bogotá a prey to the most gloomy thoughts.
All that happened eight years ago.   Be good
enough, therefore, to listen to the sequel.

Six weeks ago a letter reached me from an
old friend of Don Miguel's.   In this he informed me that my friend had been assassinated
three weeks before, and that his wife had followed him to the grave within a fortnight of

H

hearing the news. He went on to tell me that it was the Don's wish that I should be entrusted with the education of his daughter, Catalina, now a remarkably beautiful girl of between eighteen and nineteen years of age. The letter gave me to understand that she would leave the port for Bogotá by the next homeward bound mail steamer, and that she might be expected to reach Southampton on the 24th, or in other words, last Tuesday.

I should here explain that I am an old bachelor, and as such I am not accustomed to the task of entertaining young ladies. However, there was nothing for it, situated as I was, but to put a good face on the matter, and, for old sake's sake, to do what I could for my dead friend's orphan girl. My correspondent in his letter of advice had given me to understand that the young lady in question was in delicate health, but I did not expect to find such an invalid as I saw before me when I boarded the steamer in the docks. The poor girl seemed thoroughly prostrated by her grief. She did not recognise me. But I was not surprised at that, seeing that so many years had elapsed since we had last met.

From Southampton I took her home with me to my house at Ewell in Surrey, and placed her in the charge of my old housekeeper, a venerable lady, who has a peculiar but distinct faculty for managing the younger members of her sex. This, however, could not of course continue.

It became necessary for me to find some home for her where she would not only be comfortable, but where her education could be completed—for, to tell the truth, she is unusually backward for her age. It was then that I had the good fortune to hear of you, madame, hence the reason of this letter. With your kind permission I will do myself the honour of calling upon you to-morrow, Friday, at eleven a.m., in the hope of arranging some terms under which I may place my unfortunate ward, if I may so describe her, under your care. While I am upon the subject I might, with your permission, be allowed to point out that the matter of expense must be looked upon as of no object, provided always that she is made happy, that being the main object that I and my co-trustee have in view.

With the assurance of my deep respect,

Believe me to be, madame,

Sincerely yours,

GEORGE BRAMWELL TOLSON.

P.S.—Should you desire to reply to this letter in order to suggest another appointment, it would perhaps be better to do so to my private address, Thymebank Cottage, Ewell, near Epsom, as being somewhat advanced in years I seldom visit my office now.

When Miss Tibbits had finished reading, a silence fell upon the pair.

" Does it not still strike you as being in many respects peculiar? " said Miss Pinnifer at last.

" I must confess it does," replied the other lady. " It is not at all the sort of letter I should have expected the head of a large firm of London solicitors to write. Would it be considered an impertinence, my dear Miss Pinnifer, if I were to ask what action you propose taking in the matter? "

" I shall not decide until I have had an interview with the writer of the letter," answered Miss Pinnifer, with the air of a Minister Plenipotentiary about to discuss the drawing up of an international treaty. She was certainly a wonderful lady, the genus of which will very soon become extinct. She should have lived in the days of Madame Chapone and the great lexicographer. She paced the room once or twice, and then turned to Miss Tibbits again.

" Be good enough, Tibbits," said she, " to give instructions that directly Mr. Tolson arrives he shall be shown in here. I have no desire to keep him waiting."

The lady she addressed promised to attend to this, and left the room. Between ourselves, she was wondering what it was in the letter she had read that had caused her employer so much agitation. The letter was lengthy, and that it was written in a curious style for a lawyer, was true; beyond these two facts, however, there was really nothing remarkable about it, although she had pretended that she thought there was. Let us regard the case from her point of view. An elderly gentleman has a ward for whom he wishes to find a high-class school; he proposes sending her to Miss Pinnifer, and offers to pay well for the privilege of so doing. Could anything be more simple? Yet the Principal seemed to entertain a presentiment that there was something mysterious about it. Thus argued sagacious Miss Tibbits, who, like so many of her class, could be one thing to Miss Pinnifer's face and quite another behind her back. Had she but known the truth, perhaps she would have been able to understand where the real trouble lay. And here, it is only fit and proper, that I should offer an explanation.

There is an old and much worn proverb to the effect that all that glitters is not gold. It might be somewhat varied by saying that all people are not what the world supposes them to be. Miss Pinnifer was a case in point, and a remarkably sad case too. After years of patient industry she had built up for herself a connection in the scholastic line, a position second to none. She had made and put by money until she had become a moderately wealthy woman. Then the Demon of Greed, accompanied by his twin brother, the Demon of Speculation, made his appearance upon the stage, and the end was already in view. Unknown to Miss Tibbits, unknown to her lawyers, who would certainly have both counselled and cautioned her against it, she commenced to dabble on the Stock Exchange. At first she won, as is

not unfrequently the way; after a while she began
to lose with a persistency that was little short of
marvellous. Nothing she touched prospered. It
was a question of pay, pay, pay, with only the
counterfoils of her cheques to show for the money
she had staked. In an endeavour to recoup herself
she had tried other speculations, all equally risky,
and always with the same result—complete failure.
Do what she would, success would not come to
her. Fortunate in her own legitimate sphere, it
was as if Fate had determined she should not
prosper in any other. At last, and as was only
to be expected, matters arrived at such a crisis
that nothing short of ruin — ruin complete and
absolute—stared her in the face. I have been
given to understand that the spirit of gambling is
stronger in a man than in a woman, but from cases
which have come under my observation I am very
much inclined to doubt this assertion. It is a
commonplace that a woman who drinks, or who is
addicted to drugs, finds it harder to rid herself of
the habit than does a man. Be that as it may,
the wretched Miss Pinnifer found it impossible to
stop while she had the means of going on. It was
the old pitiful tale—the same which has lured so
many thousands to their ruin—" Luck *must* change
soon. It cannot go on for ever like this."

On the morning preceding the arrival of Mr.
Tolson's letter, her broker had written to inform
her that for once in a way she had been successful.
Her spirits went up immediately. Given but the
opportunity, she declared, she would regain all

that she had lost, and more besides. To do that, however, she wanted money; without capital she was like a bird with one wing clipped. She had been advised as to two excellent schemes for recouping herself, but what was the use of that if she could not avail herself of them? If only she could raise a hundred or a hundred and fifty pounds at once, it would be so easy to treble it. And there could be no doubt that this was a chance which it would be worse than folly to throw away. Never had a scheme sounded so well.

And here, doubtless, the gentle reader, like your humble servant, begins to see daylight. Here was this offer from Mr. Tolson, backed by the magic phrase " *money must be looked upon as no object.*" If only she could induce the lawyer to pay a substantial sum down she could then utilise it, possibly treble it, after which all would be well with her. Small wonder, therefore, that, coming as it did in the very nick of time, she should attach an exaggerated importance to the letter lying upon her writing-table. The question, however, was whether she could persuade him to advance so large a sum. Experience had taught her that elderly lawyers are, as a rule, a wary class, not in the least prone to generosity, particularly when dealing with other people's money. She had no less than three wards in Chancery among her pupils, and the battles that followed the presentation of each quarterly account were such as would have turned the hair of less seasoned people than Miss Pinnifer grey with worry. However, in this case there was, as I have said before, the comforting phrase set down in black and white, that pounds, shillings and pence were not to be considered of any importance in the matter.

As she stood at the window looking out upon the wet and windy-tossed square, the sound of a pupil practising in the room above came down to her. She had a professional as well as an artistic admiration for Schumann, particularly for his Sonata in D Minor, but it struck her on this occasion that there was a peculiar irony in the *scherzo* in the second movement that she had never noticed in it before. It worried her, and yet, had you asked her, I venture to believe that she could not have told you why. It had not struck her yet to think of the orphan girl who might, before very many hours were passed, be placed under her charge. All she thought of was the finding of the money which was to be invested in Patagonian Rails—as safe a speculation, so she had been informed, as anything she could dabble in, and certain for a rise. What was a mere pupil when compared with Stocks and Shares? She went back to her writing-table and sat down to indite a telegram to her broker, authorising him to purchase a certain number on the terms suggested in his letter. Already she looked upon the matter as completed, and in her mind's eye she saw the cash already standing to her credit in her banker's hands. Yet, had you called her a gambler, you would have shocked her beyond measure. She consoled herself with the idea that she was a woman of business, and the delusion comforted her. Such is not unfrequently the case.

There was a knock at the door. A maid entered.

" Mr. Tolson to see you, ma'am.".

CHAPTER VII

MR. TOLSON proved to be a dapper little man, whose age might have been anything from fifty to sixty. The top of his head was as bald and shiny as a billiard ball, the remainder was covered with snow-white hair which overlapped his collar. His face was clean-shaven, and boasted a pair of twinkling eyes that were either grey or blue, according to the light in which you looked at them. If his manner lacked something of the dignity which one is accustomed to associate with the head of a firm of world-famous solicitors, it at least made up for it in cheerfulness. One man hit him exactly when he said he reminded him of a London sparrow, inasmuch as he was always chirpy, taking everything as it came and being prepared for anything that might turn up. He was immaculately attired in a black frock-coat, and he carried the shiniest of shiny silk hats in his hand; his voice was soft and almost caressing, and his behaviour to Miss Pinnifer was gallantry itself. He advanced towards her, drawing off a grey *suède* glove as he did so.

" I can scarcely fail to be right, he said. " Madame, you are Miss Pinnifer."

" You have guessed correctly, sir," was the lady's stately reply; " I *am* Miss Pinnifer. And you are Mr. Tolson."

" George Bramwell Tolson, and very much at your service," the little man answered with a bow. He took the chair she indicated, and placed his hat on the floor by the side. " May I presume that you received my letter ? "

" It is here," said Miss Pinnifer, placing a white and still comely hand upon the sheet of notepaper on the writing-table as she spoke.

" Possibly it may have given you some cause for surprise ? "

" I must confess that on the first reading I was somewhat at a loss to understand it," she answered. " The matter, however, has become clearer to me since. I gather that the young lady, your ward, is not only an orphan, but also an invalid; that she is—ahem—if I may so express it, a little backward in her studies, and it is your desire she should become a permanent resident in my house."

" That certainly, madame, *is* my desire," he remarked, " and I sincerely trust we may be able to come to an arrangement which will be satisfactory to both parties."

Miss Pinnifer stroked her lace ruffles, and afterwards pretended to write something upon a sheet

of notepaper. So far matters were progressing
in an eminently satisfactory fashion, but she had
too much knowledge of the world to pin her faith
upon first impressions. She was thinking of
Patagonian Rails, and how she was to find the
money to purchase them.

" May I ask when you would wish the young
lady—let me see, her name is Catalina D'Araugo,
is it not ? I say, when would you wish her to take
up her residence with me ? "

" At once, madame," said the little lawyer em-
phatically. " It cannot be too soon, as far as I
am concerned. I have only to fetch her from
the hotel. She is a most charming young lady;
but, on the other hand, I am a bachelor, who has
long grown accustomed to his single life, and—
well, to cut the matter short, her presence in my
house, charming though it may be, is not altogether compatible with my idea of happiness.
Hence my visit to you."

" I understand you perfectly," exclaimed Miss
Pinnifer, who did not realise in the least what he
meant. " You would wish me to take her entirely
under my charge ? In other words, to relieve you
of all responsibility ? "

" Again you have caught my meaning exactly,"
replied Mr. Tolson; and then with a smile, he
added : " I hope you will forgive my saying so,
but such business instinct in a lady is—well, to
say the least of it, a little unusual."

Had he tried for a year he could not have paid

her a compliment she would have appreciated more. She rose to the bait as readily as a salmon rises to a March brown in April. Those Patagonian Rails seemed to be coming appreciably closer.

"I have always endeavoured to conduct my establishment on strictly business principles," she answered modestly; "but, alas, now-a-days the scholastic profession is not what it once was. The Universities and the High Schools have wrought a change which I cannot help thinking is detrimental to the best interests of our girls. When I commenced my career, the object one had in view was to make the pupil a lady in the highest sense of the word. Now-a-days, so far as I can gather, the desire is to unsex her. Grace of deportment is abandoned altogether in favour of— shall we say a desire for hockey. The art of conversation is thrown to the winds in favour of—of —well, of slang, and, if I may express it, repartee without wit."

"My dear madame, small as my experience of young ladies has been, I am quite prepared to agree with you," replied the lawyer, who was affability itself. "We live in an age of transition. I do not think, however, you will find my ward one of the class to which you refer. She has not mixed much in society. As a matter of fact, she is as unconventional a girl as I venture to believe could be discovered. Generous, warm-hearted, yet passionate to a degree. It should always be borne in mind that her father was a Spaniard, her mother a Frenchwoman, which would doubtless account for her name, Catalina, and in a measure, perhaps, for her impetuosity ! "

" I feel sure that I understand," the lady answered, playing with a paper-knife as she spoke. " She has lived a life of solitude, and now that she finds herself in the great world she is dazzled and scarcely knows her true status. However, if you will entrust her to my care, I think that you will find that I shall spare no pains to do her justice."

" I am more than sure of that, madame," replied the old gentleman with a bow. " I shall look forward to seeing a vast improvement in her when next we meet."

Miss Pinnifer was beginning to grow impatient. She wanted him to come to the point, that is to say, the question of terms, and then to take his departure as quickly as possible. This, however, seemed to be the last thing he was thinking of. He sat polishing his silk hat as if time were of no account, and yet she dared not broach the subject to him. To have done that might have been to ruin everything. But as it happened, she was not to be kept much longer in suspense, for, with a preliminary cough of apology, he turned from a discussion of the weather to that which was of such vital importance to her.

" Now, madame," he said, " if you will excuse me, we will address our attention to the matter of terms. I should, perhaps, inform you that my ward is a great heiress. We are therefore prepared to treat liberally with you, provided you will meet us on the matter of the young lady's comfort and education. Perhaps you have a prospectus that you would permit me to see."

She took one from the drawer and handed it to him. She was so nervous that she could not trust herself to speak. The old gentleman read the paper carefully. The terms were certainly most exorbitant, but he did not comment upon that fact. On the contrary, he smiled with increased affability. He really was a most extraordinary lawyer.

"Your terms will suit me admirably," he observed; "and since you will in all probability be put to some extra trouble, you will perhaps allow me to write you a cheque for half the amount in advance, with another fifty pounds wherewith to purchase anything she may require."

Miss Pinnifer felt as if she could have thrown her arms round his neck. She had scored a triumph, and the Patagonian Rails would be hers after all. Surely, she argued, this was an omen that her luck had turned and that Fortune would smile upon her after all. Summoning all her courage to her aid, she managed to falter out, "That is, of course, as you please."

Her relief may be imagined when she saw him take his cheque-book from his pocket and pick up a pen.

Two minutes later the precious draft was in her possession, and she was at work upon the receipt.

At that moment I believe she was one of the happiest women in England—if not *the* happiest.

" I will now return to the hotel and bring the young lady to you," said Mr. Tolson, rising from his chair.

" Would you not like to see the house, and particularly the apartment I shall allot to her?" asked Miss Pinnifer.

" It is not necessary," he answered with a wave of the hand. " It is Miss Pinnifer's establishment, and that fact speaks for itself."

With another low bow he turned and left the room. Had the schoolmistress been more of a woman of the world she would have repeated the remark I made just now and have said to herself, " This is really the most extraordinary lawyer I ever encountered." But she was too happy at the moment to give any thought to the matter.

Half an hour later a cab drove up to the door, and Mr. Tolson slipped out of it and gave his hand to a young lady dressed entirely in black. She was unusually tall, and possessed of a fine figure—moreover she carried herself with a grace which was probably attributable to her Southern origin. Judged from a distance, she seemed somewhat advanced to become a pupil at a boarding school, but as we have already seen, that has been satisfactorily accounted for. It has been said that there were times when the proprietress of Athena House, Senlac Square, could give evidence of the fact that she was possessed of a temper of her own; on this occasion, however, she was affability itself. She received the young lady with almost motherly kindness, hoped she would be happy, and told her that if there was anything she wanted she must be sure to ask for it, when it should be immediately forthcoming. It was then, for the first time, that the peculiarity of the girl's manner became apparent. She seemed scarcely conscious of her actions, and as Miss Pinnifer declared afterwards, gave her the impression of being more like a somnambulist than a young lady in the full possession of her senses. When addressed, she answered in monosyllables, and appeared not to take the slightest interest in her surroundings. Miss Pinnifer rang the bell and bade the maid who answered it summon Miss Tibbits to her presence.

"My dear Miss Tibbits," said she, "will you be good enough to conduct Miss D'Araugo to her apartment and see that she wants for nothing."

When they were alone together the lawyer said in a low voice : "You can now see for yourself, my dear madame, the despondent state of mind to which her bereavement has reduced her. I have no doubt, however, that under your fostering care, it will not be very long before she is herself again. Now, with your permission, I will take leave of you. Should you desire to communicate with me you have my address."

"Do you not wish to say 'good-bye' to your ward?" asked the lady in some surprise.

He shook his head and informed her that that operation had already been performed in the cab. He once more bowed himself out, stepped into the cab, and drove away, leaving the school-dame more convinced than ever that the whole affair was one of the most extraordinary that she had ever known in her life.

It is not permitted to ordinary males to become familiar with the workings of a young ladies' Seminary, but it may be taken for granted that the newcomer did not escape criticism from her school - fellows. Her pronunciation, with its foreign accent, her dark hair and eyes, the small- ness of her hands and feet, were the envy of some and the admiration of all, but what struck everyone was her curiously listless manner; as when she had arrived she appeared to take no interest in anything, her thoughts seemed to be miles and miles away. If spoken to, some time elapsed before she replied, and then it was only as if she were doing so out of mere politeness. Later in the evening Miss Pinnifer paid her the extreme honour of inviting her to accompany her to her *sanctum sanctorum*.

" My dear," she said when they reached it, " I want you to look upon me as a friend, one whom you can trust and to whom you must always come should you be in any trouble or difficulty. I have had great experience with girls, as you may sup- pose, and as your guardian has placed you entirely in my care, I feel that it is my duty to do all that lies in my power, not only to promote your happiness, but also to see that you come to no harm. I hope you feel that you can place your trust in me?"

The girl, however, showed no enthusiasm or indeed any gratitude for this kindly speech. She merely murmured her thanks, and after that sat as silent as before.

"I hope you understand what I mean," continued Miss Pinnifer, somewhat chagrined at the undemonstrative reception with which her offer had been met. It was not often that she made such overtures, but when she did she expected them to be received with the gratitude she felt they merited.

"I think it is only fair that I should tell you that your painful story has been made known to me. You have suffered greatly, but I pray that your troubles are now at an end and that happier days are in store for you."

For one brief moment the other showed some signs of animation. A look that was one of almost terror came into her face, and she shrank away from the old lady as if she thought that she was about to do her some grievous bodily harm. Then it all changed again and she became as impassive as before. Thinking that perhaps she was tired after her journey, Miss Pinnifer dispatched her to bed at an early hour. The faithful Tibbits attended her, by her superior's orders, and partly in the hope that she might learn something more about her. Curiosity was one of that lady's strongest characteristics. But she was not destined to learn anything, for far from being communicative, the girl scarcely spoke. So, having done all she could for her, Miss Tibbits bade her " goodnight " and took her departure. Later on she discussed the new pupil with one of the governesses and gave it as her opinion that she was not quite right in her mind.

" And it seems a great pity too," said Miss Tibbits, " for she is a pretty young lady as I have ever seen, and carries herself with an air that is truly *distingué*."

Miss Pinnifer's factotum rather prided herself on the elegance of her conversation. She endeavoured to imitate her employer in all things, perhaps on the principle that imitation is said to be the sincerest form of flattery.

At last the house was shut up for the night, and silence reigned throughout the building. Doubtless Miss Pinnifer dreamt of success with Patagonian Rails, Miss Tibbits of her multifarious household duties, the French governess of her home on the outskirts of Paris—but what did Catalina D'Araugo dream of, or did she dream at all ? "

The clock of the church in the next square had just struck one, and according to her own account, as explained to Tibbits, Miss Pinnifer was entering upon her second sleep, when a piercing shriek rang through the building. It was repeated again and again.

"Good gracious, what is that?" said the schoolmistress to herself, and next moment she was donning her dressing-gown preparatory to going forth to find out. "Is it somebody being murdered or am I dreaming?"

Taking up her candle, she hurried into the corridor, where she found Miss Tibbits, several of the governesses, and some of the pupils huddled together like a flock of frightened sheep.

"Go back to your apartments, all of you," she said sternly, "with the exception of Miss Tibbits. Tibbits, come with me, I must find out what this means."

She had scarcely spoken before the shriek rang out again, this time even louder than before. Then a girl's voice, which they immediately recognised, cried something in Spanish.

"It is Miss D'Araugo," ejaculated Tibbits, as if the fact were not apparent to her employer. "She must be suffering from nightmare."

Miss Pinnifer did not deign to answer, but strode along the corridor in the direction of the new pupil's room. Even in her dressing-gown and her frilled night-cap, the mistress of Athena House could still manage to look dignified. Arriving at the girl's room, she paused for a moment at the door, and then, turning the handle, entered, Miss Tibbits following close behind her. It was a strange scene they had presented to them. The new pupil was standing in the middle of the floor in what was apparently an agony of terror. Her hands were clenched and her whole figure trembled under the intensity of her emotion. Again she shrieked and again she cried something in Spanish. Though it was evident to her audience that she was not conscious of what she was doing, her eyes were wide open. Miss Pinnifer approached her and laid her hand upon her arm.

"My poor child," she said, "what does all this mean? What is the matter? Are you ill?"

Without giving any sign of being startled, the girl turned to her and said in a low, eager voice, and in English:

"They're following me. I saw him to-day. If I am not careful they will catch me yet."

"No, no, you are only dreaming, child," said the old lady. "Believe me, no one is following you. You are quite safe. Go back to your bed, my dear, and you may be quite sure that I will not allow anyone to harm you."

Without another word the girl did as she was bid, and, if appearances counted for anything, her eyes closed and she was fast asleep almost before her head touched the pillow. The two other women stood looking down at her for some minutes, then satisfied that she was safe, they quietly left the room. Once outside, Miss Pinnifer beckoned her subordinate to her own apartment and bade her close the door.

"This is very extraordinary, Tibbits," she said. "I cannot understand it. Was she awake or asleep, do you think, when we entered?"

" Asleep, I should venture to say," answered the other. " Possibly she may be a somnambulist."

" That may be so, but her eyes were certainly open. Can she have any reason for believing she is being followed, or was it merely a dream ? "

" I should be inclined to suppose the latter. Who would be likely to follow her ? "

" Pray bear in mind the fact that her poor father was assassinated. Is it not more than likely that she may be haunted by the idea that the man who committed the crime intends the same fate for herself ? One is familiar with the fiery natures of these South Americans."

" Very true, very true," replied the other, with the air of one who has made the Spanish-American character her especial study. " As you say, her behaviour may be attributable to that cause. Without a doubt, that terrible event must have been a serious shock to her—poor girl."

" Serious, indeed; and now, Tibbits, you had better return to your own apartment. Should we have a repetition of the scene we have just witnessed I beg that you will again accompany me to her chamber. And, by the way, Tibbits, you might look in upon her to-morrow morning about seven o'clock, and report to me as to her condition. I shall be most anxious to hear."

Miss Tibbits promised to do so, and retired to her own room. Once more silence reigned in the house.

Faithful to her promise, the lady in question entered the new pupil's room precisely at seven o'clock, taking with her a cup of tea, that feminine panacea for all ills. She approached the bed with it, and having done so, almost dropped the cup and saucer in her amazement. She found it difficult to believe the evidence of her own eyes.

The bed was empty, and there was no sign of the young lady to be seen.

Miss Tibbits looked about the room, behind the curtains, and even under the bed, but without discovering any trace of the girl she sought.

" Good gracious," muttered the astonished lady, " can this be true? Whatever will Miss Pinnifer say? " She trembled when she thought of it. The situation was too awful to be contemplated. She hastened to the window, only to find that it was securely fastened. It was evident that she had not used that as a means of exit. There was nothing for it, she argued, but to go and inform her principal without delay. She accordingly made her way to the latter's room in fear and trembling. It was then that she did a thing which, under other circumstances, she would not have believed possible, that is to say, she entered the august presence without the formality of knocking on the door. In spite of what had happened earlier, the proprietress of Athena House was fast asleep. For a moment Miss Tibbits paused, scarcely knowing what to do. Even in a moment of such grave anxiety, her

respect for that omnipotent lady held her en-
thralled. She met the difficulty half way by
coughing gently. This, however, proved in-
effective, so she coughed once more—again without
arousing her.

"This is terrible," she muttered to herself,
"Whatever shall I do?"

Plainly there was only one course open to her,
and that was so overwhelming that she scarcely
dared to contemplate it. Imagine the feelings of
a Page of Honour if he were called upon to take
the Czar of All the Russias by the shoulder and
shake him into wakefulness. If you can picture
that you will be able to understand something of
how the luckless lady felt at that moment. Summoning up all her courage, she advanced to the
bed and said in a voice that she scarcely recognised: "Miss Pinnifer, Miss Pinnifer," but Miss
Pinnifer still slept on. At last, well nigh driven
to despair, she took her employer by the shoulders
and gave her half a turn. A moment later she
was clinging to the brass rail of the bedstead in
a state of semi-consciousness. Then her hold
gradually relaxed, and she fell in a dead faint
upon the floor. How long she remained in this
condition she cannot remember. But when she
came to her senses she found it difficult to realise
that she was lying upon the floor of Miss Pinnifer's
bedroom. Sick and dizzy, she struggled to her
feet, and, as she did so, the remembrance of what
she had seen came back to her with all its ghastly

reality. Once more she approached the bed, though how she managed to do so she did not even know herself. Alas! it was no dream—it was only too true. Miss Pinnifer had been brutally murdered. Her throat had been cut from ear to ear.

CHAPTER VIII

IT is quite beyond the scope of my ability to give you any adequate idea of the state of poor Miss Tibbits' feelings when she realised the dreadful fate which had befallen her unfortunate mistress. The only expression I can find that at all fits the case would be to say that she was paralysed for the time being. She stood staring at the terrible figure on the bed as if she could not withdraw her eyes from it. For the moment she did not attempt to understand what it meant to her. In spite of the other's overbearing manner and the way she had sometimes treated her, she had been genuinely attached to Miss Pinnifer. Now her feelings were too numbed by the shock she had received to be able to realise that the other had gone out of her life for ever. At last, little by little, her senses returned to her, and she felt that it behoved her to do something. Scarcely knowing what she was doing, she tottered from the room, softly closing the door behind her, as if she feared by making any noise she might wake the sleeper on the bed.

Stepping quietly, she made her way to the hall, where she found one of the maids at work. Her she dispatched to the English governess, a staid, middle-aged lady for whom she entertained a great respect. With a presumption upon which she would never at any other time have ventured, she awaited the latter's coming in the murdered woman's own sanctum. How familiar it all was, and yet how different it seemed now, the writing-table with its orderly array of pens, paper and ink; the book-case with its collection of calf-bound classics, which I fear were seldom read; the photographs of byegone pupils upon the mantelpiece; and all the hundred and one little knick-knacks that a woman gets together in the course of a prosperous career. Looking at that well-known chair before the writing-table, she could almost imagine that she could see the old lady seated in it, bolt upright, clad in her black gown, her grey curls balancing the somewhat stern but not altogether unkindly face. And to think that she—but no, she dared not think of that. If she did she believed she would go mad.

Then the door opened and Miss Tuckett, the English governess, entered the room. She was a stout, matronly individual, as phlegmatic as the proverbial Dutchman, in fact, just the person to advise and to lean upon in such a crisis.

" Good gracious, Miss Tibbits," she began, as she saw the other's face. " What is the matter? Are you ill? Let me ring for the housekeeper, that she may bring you some brandy."

Without waiting for the other to reply she rang the bell and gave the necessary order. When a stiff dose of the spirit had been administered, the unfortunate Miss Tibbits somewhat revived.

" Now for goodness sake collect your wits and try to tell me what is the matter," said the practical Miss Tuckett. " It is not often you give way like this."

" I can't help it, I can't help it," moaned the other. " I have lost my good mistress, and I shall never see her like again."

For once in her life the English governess showed signs of being startled.

" What do you mean, woman; have you gone mad ? "

" I wish I had," sobbed the other, without heeding the term " woman," which, at any other time, she would have bitterly resented. " But it is quite true what I am telling you. She is dead, she has been foully murdered." Here she threw up her hands and fell to rocking herself backwards and forwards in her chair in what was apparently a paroxysm of grief. Miss Tuckett fell upon her and shook her as one shakes a naughty child.

" I don't believe a word of it," she cried; " you are dreaming." But there was an expression upon her face as she said it which showed that she was not altogether as sceptical as she pretended to be.

" It's as true as that I am sitting here," answered the other, suddenly ceasing her moaning under the stimulus of contradiction. " If you do not believe me, come and see for yourself."

Together the two women went upstairs and entered the death chamber. Less than a moment sufficed to convince the English governess that what she had been told was, unhappily, only too correct.

"But who can have been wicked enough to do it?" she asked in a horrified whisper. "So far as I know she had no enemies, at least, not one who would be likely to commit such a dastardly deed."

"Come with me again," said Miss Tibbits, and she led her to the room which had been occupied by the new pupil.

"Where is she?" asked the English governess as she looked about her in surprise.

"Gone," replied the other. "I took her up a cup of tea at seven o'clock, according to Miss Pinnifer's instructions, and found the room empty. Do you know what I think? I think that she was mad, and that it was she who murdered my poor mistress. Having done so, she ran away."

The English governess looked grave, as well she might. It was a serious charge to bring against the girl; but there was no gainsaying the fact that things looked very black against her. She had behaved so strangely on the preceding night, that anyone would have felt justified in believing, as Miss Tibbits had said, that she was not quite right in her mind. Her curious behaviour in the middle of the night added to, rather than detracted from, the weight of suspicion against her.

"And now what are we to do?" asked the younger woman.

"We must communicate with the police without delay," said Miss Tuckett, the practical, "and also with Mr. Penfold, her lawyer. They will take charge of the matter. There will have to be an inquest, and the detectives will have to try to find the murderer."

"Or murderess," put in Miss Tibbits vindictively. "Nothing will ever convince me that that girl did not commit the crime. Oh, my poor, kind mistress, that you should have met with such a fate. It is too cruel—too cruel."

Miss Tibbits was one of that large class of persons who are able to discover more virtues in a person after death than they ever dreamt of during life.

"We had better lock both the doors, and you keep the keys until the police arrive," said Miss Tuckett, who by this time had quite regained that common-sense which was one of her chief characteristics.

The doors of the two rooms were accordingly locked and the keys deposited safely in Miss Tibbits' capacious pocket.

"Now I shall go for the police myself," remarked the English governess, as if it were the most natural thing in the world for her to do. "In cases like this there should be no delay."

The other envied her her spirit, and began to feel that, after all, she herself was a poor, weak creature.

" And the young ladies," she asked, " what are we to do about them ? "

" For the present they must be kept in ignorance of what has happened. We shall be compelled to communicate with their parents later on, I suppose. Now I am going. Give the maids to understand that their mistress is not well and does not wish to be disturbed. That will account for the door being locked."

Miss Tibbits promised to attend to these details, and the other departed on her errand.

A quarter of an hour later an inspector of police, accompanied by a doctor, and a constable, made his appearance at the house, and had an interview with trembling Miss Tibbits in her late mistress's *sanctum sanctorum*. From her lips he heard all that she knew of the tragedy, punctuated by sobs. She described the arrival of the new pupil on the previous day, her singular behaviour during the night, and the fact that she was missing in the morning.

" At what time did you last see the deceased alive ? " asked the inspector, tapping his note-book with his pencil.

" About half-past one o'clock," the woman replied.

" Where was that, may I ask ? These particulars are all of importance."

" In her own apartment," was the answer.

" Was that after or before the scene you describe as having taken place in the new pupil's room ? " was the next question.

" It was after it," answered Miss Tibbits. " She desired to consult me about it."

" You say that the young lady, who was brought here by her guardian, a lawyer, struck everyone as being peculiar in her manner? Be so good as to describe her peculiarity to me as nearly as you can."

Miss Tibbits' spirits revived at once. She saw a chance of being vindictive, and hastened to avail herself of it.

" She was morose," she said; " would scarcely speak to anyone, and when she did it was only to say ' yes ' or ' no.' She came from South America, but I wouldn't trust anyone who came from those parts with anything. It's my belief they'd as soon murder you as look at you. If this girl didn't murder my poor mistress, I don't know who did."

" Never mind that," put in the inspector, who did not wish to waste time. " She may have done so or she may not. What I want are the facts as far as you are able to give them to me. By the way, did the young lady in question leave any luggage behind her? "

" Two boxes," was the reply.

" Then she took nothing with her? "

" Nothing, so far as I can tell," said Miss Tibbits.

" Were the doors and windows securely fastened downstairs? "

" I attended to them myself," was the rejoinder given with some little asperity.

K

"And were they fastened this morning?"

Miss Tibbits was compelled to confess that she had made no enquiry on the subject.

"Never mind," said the inspector, "we can enquire about that later. Now, if you please, we will go upstairs.

As they left the sanctum and entered the hall the front door was opened by a maidservant, and the English governess entered, followed by a tall, elderly gentleman, with a thin, hatchet-like face, decorated with a pair of long grey whiskers. This was Mr. Penfold, Miss Pinnifer's lawyer.

"Good morning, Inspector; good morning, Doctor," he began. Then, turning to Miss Tibbits, "This is an extremely bad business. I don't know when I have been more shocked."

Before she could well reply, the inspector interposed with :

"We were about to go upstairs, Mr. Penfold; perhaps you would be good enough to accompany us?"

"I suppose I had better," was the answer. "But I must confess that I do not look forward to doing so."

They accordingly ascended the stairs to the room in which the unfortunate victim of the tragedy lay.

"My poor client," said the lawyer as he looked at her. "How little did I imagine that this would be your end."

There could be no doubt that the old gentleman was genuinely grieved. The doctor approached the bed and made his examination. It was not a long one.

" It is needless for me to tell you," he said, " that she is dead."

" In your opinion how long is it since death took place ? " asked the lawyer.

" Roughly speaking, I should say from five to seven hours."

" You will, of course, be subpœned for the inquest," remarked the inspector.

" I presume I shall have no option," the other replied. " You do not want me any more now, I suppose ? "

" No, thank you. I am much obliged to you, Doctor. Good morning."

The medical man left the room, whereupon the inspector began his examination of the apartment. There were two or three spots of blood on the carpet near the door, and another on the vallence of the bed. He pointed them out to the lawyer, who enquired what construction he placed upon it.

" Well, in my opinion," the other replied, " it points conclusively to the fact that the murder was not committed in the room, but elsewhere. The next question is to find out where."

They left the room and passed into the corridor outside. It was lighted by a window at the further end, but this was not sufficient for the inspector's purpose. He therefore asked Miss Tibbits to be good enough to furnish him with a candle. When this was forthcoming, he went down on his hands and knees and made a patient examination of the carpet near the door, and another on the valance the left, that is to say, towards the hall and main staircase, there was nothing to be seen. He therefore turned his attention to the right.

" Yes, here it is," he said. " Spot number one." Further on there was another, and so on until at last they reached the door of the room which had been occupied by the new pupil.

" There, what did I tell you ? " cried Miss Tibbits triumphantly. " Did I not say that it was she who committed the crime ? I felt sure of it from the first."

Neither of the men answered, but the inspector opened the door and entered the room. Everything was just as the girl had left it; nothing had been disturbed. Her two boxes stood on either side of the wardrobe; the bed-clothes lay in disorder on the bed, her articles of toilet were upon the dressing-table, and the shoes she had worn on the previous evening were side by side beneath it, but, strange to say, sign of blood there was none.

" That is very extraordinary," said the inspector, rising to his feet once more. " Very extraordinary indeed. The blood comes up to the door, but there is no sign of it in here. If the murder had been committed outside the door there would have been ample evidence of the fact. As it is, there are only a few spots of blood. Common-sense tells us that the unfortunate lady could not have walked up here and back again with her throat cut. I fancy it promises to be one of the most extraordinary cases that I have known during my experience of crime."

" Pardon my making a suggestion," put in the lawyer. "But is not the theory of suicide permissible."

The police officer shook his head.

" In the first place, though as you saw I searched carefully, I could find no instrument with which such an act could have been effected. Then again, you have the blood stains in the corridor to account for. No, my dear sir, with all due respect to you, the suicide theory will not hold water."

The lawyer scratched his chin with his thumb.

"In that case," he replied, "I am equally at a loss with you to understand it. And what do you propose doing now?"

" To begin with, we must endeavour to find the girl, and the coroner must be communicated with. It would be as well, I should say, if you were to telegraph to the gentleman who placed her under Miss Pinnifer's care. It is within the bounds of possibility that she has returned to him, though personally I do not think it likely. If she were guilty she would know that that would be the first place where we should look for her. As it is, that is what we shall do. I will now lock the rooms and take the keys with me. The man I have brought with me will remain in charge."

" In the meantime I will telegraph to Mr.—let me see, I think you said his name was Tolson— to Mr. Tolson and make him acquainted with the terrible news. I know him very well by repute, and I am quite sure that he will be as shocked as I am when he hears it. The firm is one of the most respected in the profession."

The doors were locked and the constable placed in charge, after which the police officer took his departure. By this time the news that something was wrong had spread through the house, and the young ladies were in such a state, which could only be described as one of absolute terror. They could not remain in the house, one and all declared. Nothing would induce them to leave the lower regions or to venture anywhere near that terrible corridor.

In despair, the English governess, who by right of seniority had taken over control, approached the lawyer on the subject, and asked him as one of Miss Pinnifer's executors as well as her lawyer, what was the best to be done.

"Telegraph to their parents and send them home," was the prompt reply. "It is not the least use their remaining here. As a matter of fact they will only be in the way."

Telegrams were accordingly dispatched, and in due course the girls departed to their respective abodes. Shortly after lunch, Mr. Penfold again put in an appearance. He had received a telegram from Mr. Tolson, in which he said that he was leaving by the next train for Brighton. As yet he only knew that his ward was missing; nothing had been told him of the murder, Mr. Penfold having deemed it more prudent to acquaint him of the fact on his arrival. Meanwhile the police were searching in every direction through the town for the missing girl, but so far without success. The constable whose beat included the square had been examined, and he was positive that he had seen nothing of her. They made enquiries at the various railway stations within a considerable distance of the town—but still no news. Nothing could be heard of her. She might have vanished into thin air for any trace of her the police could discover.

Towards three o'clock Mr. Tolson put in an appearance. It was easy to see as he descended from the cab that he was in an agitated frame of mind; his usually jovial face was clouded over with care, and he looked years older than when he had done on the previous day. Miss Tibbits opened the door to him herself, and in the hall he discovered a tall, elderly gentleman, whose very appearance betokened the fact that he was of the same profession as himself. The latter advanced to meet him.

"Mr. Tolson, I believe," he said. "May I introduce myself? My name is Penfold, and I am Miss Pinnifer's legal adviser, or perhaps I should say I was."

"But surely, my dear sir, there is no need for us to make this unhappy circumstance a legal affair," remarked the newcomer. "If the unhappy girl has run away, I am quite sure Miss Pinnifer is not to blame. I can assure you, I entertain the highest respect for her integrity."

" Perhaps it would be as well if we were to discuss the matter elsewhere. We will go into the dining-room, and perhaps, Miss Tibbits, you will be good enough to see that we are not disturbed.''

Such was Miss Tibbits' curiosity that she would willingly have followed them into the room, but the way in which Mr. Penfold closed the door showed her very plainly that he would not permit such a thing. Worse than all, the arrival of the English and French governesses on the scene precluded any possibility of her listening at the keyhole. She felt that this was hard, seeing what an important part she had played in the case.

When the door had been closed the two men walked to the window at the further end of the room and seated themselves there. The window looked out over a garden at the back, in which the pupils had been wont to disport themselves in happier days. The view was not altogether a cheerful one; it had that indescribable boarding school air that one is never able quite to dissociate from even the most high-class educational establishments, such as Miss Pinnifer's undoubtedly was. The grass of the lawn had been worn away in many places by dainty young feet, the trees and shrubs appeared to be ashamed of their surroundings, while the very brick wall which surrounded it seemed suggestive of a prison. For a few moments both men sat watching it in silence. The Brighton lawyer was thinking of the dead woman upstairs, and wondering how he was to enter upon his tale; his London *confrère* was thinking of his ward and wondering what had induced her to take such an extraordinary step as to run away. If the truth must be told, both were undeniably ill at ease, and, all things considered, it is scarcely to be wondered at that they were. Mr. Tolson was the first to break the silence. His remark, however, was scarcely original—he had made it, or something very like it, before.

" This is a very sad business," he began, " and not only sad, but an extremely annoying one for everyone concerned. I cannot say personally when I have been more annoyed by anything. At my age such things affect one more than they do the younger men."

" It has given me a shock such as I have never known before," replied Mr. Penfold, forgetting for the moment that the other as yet knew nothing of the tragedy which had befallen the house.

Mr. Tolson gazed at him in some surprise. Since he was merely Miss Pinnifer's legal adviser it seemed strange to him that he should take the matter so much to heart. He did not comment on the fact, however; he had enough to think of without doing that.

" I had quite thought that the foolish girl would have settled down happily here," he continued. " She would have had companions of her own age or nearly so, to associate with, a comfortable home, combined with the best of opportunities for improving her education, which, as you have doubtless heard, was, to say the least of it, extremely backward. Instead of which, she must needs run away before she has been in the house twenty-four hours. I presume you have caused enquiries to be made for her?"

"The police have the matter in hand, and are searching everywhere for her," answered Mr. Penfold. "It will be strange if they don't find her before very long. A girl of such singular beauty and alone could scarcely fail to attract attention. If she did not take train to London, and the railway people feel confident that she did not, she cannot have had time to get very far. Personally, my opinion is that she is wandering on the Downs."

"Poor soul, I trust she will come to no harm there," put in Mr. Tolson. "I would not have anything happen to her for the wealth of all the Indies. Not so much for her own sake, perhaps, as for the sake of another, who is very dear to me. Ah! my dear sir, if only you knew all the ins and outs of this affair, I know you would feel as I do about it."

"I know enough to make me feel very sad," the other rejoined bitterly. "I know that she has in all human probability lost me an old friend and a respected client. I have acted for Miss Pinnifer for nearly thirty years, and, as one of the profession, you will know what that means."

"But surely the loss of one pupil cannot make much difference to a lady of Miss Pinnifer's standing in her profession," said Mr. Tolson.

" Even if, after all, the pupil is lost to her. Besides, who knows but what I may be able to induce her to forgive the reckless girl and to take her back into her house ? "

" Miss Pinnifer will take no more pupils," said Mr. Penfold gloomily.

" What do you mean ? "

The other paused for a moment before he replied.

" I mean that Miss Pinnifer was foully murdered in the early hours of this morning, and that since that time your ward has been missing."

CHAPTER IX

Mr. Tolson sat and looked at Mr. Penfold with a face that was consternation itself. He tried to speak, but at the first attempt his voice failed him. He could not utter a sound. At last he recovered himself somewhat.

"Good heavens, my dear sir," he cried in tones of horror, "is it possible that what you say can be true? Miss Pinnifer murdered—I cannot believe it. It seems incredible. Who can have committed such a dastardly crime?"

It was evident from this speech that he had not properly realised the true purport of the communication the other had made to him. How to make him see it without giving him unnecessary pain was the problem the Brighton lawyer was called upon to solve, and he found it difficult to do so. Nearly half a minute must have elapsed before he answered.

"You must prepare yourself for some bad news, Mr. Tolson," he said, and then came to a sudden stop. He devoutly wished himself anywhere but where he was.

"Is there more bad news for me to hear?" asked the old man. "Surely I have heard enough. Miss Pinnifer murdered, and my ward missing—that should be enough for any man, in all conscience."

"Can you not understand even now?" asked the other, almost testily, for his nerves were undergoing a severe strain and they reacted on his temper. "Surely you can guess without putting me to the pain of having to tell you."

"How can I guess when I have not the least idea of what you are driving at?" replied Mr. Tolson with corresponding petulance. "If you would only be good enough to explain yourself, it would save both of us much time and worry. Speak out, sir, and be done with it."

"In that case there is nothing for it but for me to tell you. Don't blame me, however, if the telling causes you pain. Miss Pinnifer, as I have already told you, has been brutally murdered, and your ward has disappeared. Can you see no connection between the two events?"

Mr. Tolson sprang from his chair with a cry.

"Good God!" he shouted, "you don't mean to tell me that you believe her guilty of the murder?"

"I am only too sorry to say that the weight of evidence seems to point in that direction," retorted Mr. Penfold. "Look at it calmly. From what I can gather there can be little or no doubt that the young lady in question is—well—she is not quite as strong in her mind as she might be. Everyone remarked it. It was the talk of the establishment last night."

"A fig for the talk of the establishment," cried the irate lawyer. "I tell you the thing is absurd, ridiculous, monstrous. I knew the girl's father and mother, and I have known her since she was an infant. She has seen great trouble, and it has brought about a species of melancholia, that is all. She is as incapable of such an act as you would accuse her of as you are yourself. Dismiss such a suspicion from your mind at once, I implore you."

"I wish I could," the other answered with a shake of his head. "Alas! however, it is impossible. At the risk of displeasing you, I must say that the facts are too patent to be disputed. She behaved in a most extraordinary manner last night — shrieked and complained that she was being followed by people, and acted altogether in a most peculiar manner."

"But I tell you again, sir, that the thing is absurd, that it is not to be thought of. I am prepared to pledge my own reputation that she is innocent. There is some hideous mistake. As for her saying that she was being followed, I can explain that quite easily. She has never been the same girl since her father's assassination and her poor mother's death. The terrible scene is always before her, and her constant fear is that she is being followed by the assassin and that she will meet the same unhappy fate as befell them. Small wonder is it, therefore, that she is depressed. That was one of my chief reasons for desiring to place her under Miss Pinnifer's care. I thought that the discipline of the school and the companionship of the other pupils might have a salutary effect upon her. It would appear, however, that I was mistaken. The pity was that I ever brought her here at all."

He spoke with such bitterness that Mr. Penfold felt even sorrier for him than before. But what was to be done? He was by this time as convinced as was Miss Tibbits that the girl had committed the murder, and however willing he might be to think otherwise he could not do so against his better judgment. As a man of the world and as a lawyer, that would have been too absurd. While he was thinking of this the inspector of police was announced, and was introduced to Mr. Tolson.

" I understand that you have been searching for my unfortunate ward," said the latter. " Have you any news of her? "

" None whatever," was the curt reply. Then, after a short pause, he added, " We have men out in every direction hunting for her, and all the stations within a large radius have been warned to keep a sharp lookout. But when I left headquarters a quarter of an hour ago no news had been received of her."

" Tell me, Mr. Inspector," said the old gentleman, " that is to say if it is consistent with your duty to do so, whether, after what you have seen and have been told of the case, you believe her to be guilty of this atrocious charge?"

"At present I cannot tell you what I think," the officer answered, "inasmuch as I do not know myself. It is a most complicated case, and one is afraid to say anything until more details are brought to light. A man from Scotland Yard will come down to-night to commence investigations, and then perhaps we may come to some better understanding of it. At present we are, so to speak, almost in the dark. If we could find a motive, the rest should be comparatively easy. But so far as we have been able to discover nothing has been taken, yet on the other hand, it cannot be found that Miss Pinnifer had an enemy in the world—certainly not one who would be likely to enter her house and murder her in the middle of the night."

"In searching for a motive, would it facilitate matters at all if I were to inform you that yesterday I drew a cheque in Miss Pinnifer's favour for two hundred and fifty pounds? Might not this have been some inducement to an assassin to take her life? The idea is feasible."

"It is possible that it might—though in my opinion, not probable," replied the inspector. "If the cheque is gone and has not been presented at the bank the circumstance might be worthy of consideration."

"Can we not settle that point once and for all?" asked Mr. Penfold, who had not spoken for some time. " Miss Tibbits should be able to tell us where the deceased lady was in the habit of keeping her money, and we could then satisfy ourselves as to whether it is there or not. An enquiry at the bank will set the other matter at rest. What do you say, Inspector ? "

" There can be no harm in trying it," he replied. "Where can we find Miss — the lady you mention ? "

" I will call her," said Mr. Penfold, and left the room in search of Miss Tibbits. When he returned with her the inspector put the question to her. Her reply was to the effect that to the best of her belief the deceased lady kept any money she might have in the house, in one of the drawers of the writing-table in her own sanctum. The key was thereupon obtained, and the three men entered the apartment together, only to discover that they wanted the key of the writing-table before they could commence operations. Enquiry of Miss Tibbits went to show that Miss Pinnifer had been for many years in the habit of carrying them about with her, and that in all probability they were in the pocket of the dress she had worn on the previous evening. This proved to be the case.

The keys being forthcoming, the desk was opened by the inspector, one of the lawyers being seated on either side of him. The various drawers were filled almost to overflowing with papers, and Mr. Penfold's face became grave as roll after roll of worthless scrip came to light. While he was aware that his unfortunate client had speculated

L

a great deal, he had no idea that it was so heavily or in such wild-cat stock. The top drawer having been drawn blank, the others were opened in their turn and examined carefully. But search where they would, they could discover no trace of what they wanted. Without a doubt she must have posted the draft to the bank soon after she had received it. The only thing to be done, therefore, was to enquire at the bank with as little delay as possible. A cab was accordingly called, and in it the three gentlemen drove to the institution in question. Both Mr. Penfold and the inspector were well known, and in consequence they experienced no difficulty in obtaining admission, for it was after closing time, and also an interview with the manager. He was a portly, dignified gentleman, as befitted his calling, who took his position seriously, as well he might. When Mr. Tolson had been introduced to him he invited them to be seated.

"And what can I have the pleasure of doing for you, gentlemen," he asked, playing with his gold-rimmed glasses as he spoke. " I regret that I cannot spare you very much time, but the fact is I have a Board meeting in a quarter of an hour, and as you are aware, Directors, like Time and Tide, wait for no man."

He chuckled at his own small joke, and then, leaning back in his chair, waited to learn their business with him. When he heard that his old customer, Miss Pinnifer, had been murdered, he was genuinely shocked.

"But may I ask in what way I am interested in the matter?" he enquired after he had expressed his horror and sympathy. "I do not quite see in what way we, that is, the bank, is implicated."

"Yesterday, this gentleman, Mr. Tolson," explained the inspector, "handed the deceased lady a cheque for two hundred and fifty pounds. We have been searching for it at the house, but have been quite unable to find it. Our object in calling upon you is to discover whether or not the draft in question has been presented."

The manager rang the bell upon his writing-table and bade the clerk who answered it request the head cashier to come to him.

"Mr. Soames," he said, when that gentleman made his appearance, "have you received a cheque drawn by Mr. Tolson in favour of Miss Pinnifer, of Senlac Square?"

"Yes, sir," the cashier replied; "it was paid in this morning, together with a cheque drawn by Miss Pinnifer herself for two hundred pounds in favour of a Mr. Archibald Wilkinson."

"Ah!" said Mr. Tolson, "this is beginning to grow interesting. Might I ask at what time they were presented?"

"As soon as we opened," was the prompt reply.

"Might we see them?"

"With pleasure," answered the manager. "Be good enough to bring them in, Mr. Soames, will you?"

The two documents were presently forthcoming. The inspector examined them first and then handed them on to Mr. Penfold, remarking as he did so that he must be familiar with his client's signature.

" So far as I can tell the signatures on the face of one and the back of the other are in her hand-writing—but of course I cannot speak positively. What do you think, Mr. Soames? "

The cashier gave it as his opinion that there could be no sort of doubt on the subject. In proof of it he had honoured the cheque in favour of Mr. Wilkinson without a second thought.

" Have you any other cheques drawn by her within the last fortnight? " enquired the inspector. " If so, I should be glad if you would let me see them. I should like to make a comparison."

Several returned drafts were presently forth-coming and the police officer spread them out upon the manager's desk and studied them carefully for some minutes. At last he turned to the manager and said :

" I most firmly believe the cheque drawn in favour of this man Wilkinson, or whatever his real name may be, to be a forgery. If you will place it beside any of the others I feel sure you will be able to detect the difference. For instance, in all the other cheques where the word ' Mr.' occurs you will notice that the ' M ' invariably slopes to the left, while here it slopes to the right, a sudden change which such a precise old lady would be scarcely to make after so many years. Again, if you will examine the capital letter in ' Pinnifer ' you will notice that in the other twelve cheques the down stroke is so fine as to be almost illegible, yet here it is as heavy as if it had been written by a rough man with a J pen. And last, but not least, does it not strike you as being highly improbable that a lady of Miss Pinnifer's business-like habits would draw a cheque in favour of 'bearer' and for such a large amount as two hundred pounds?"

"I can scarcely credit it," remarked Mr. Penfold, who was naturally familiar with his late client's idiosyncrasies. "Pray, what sort of man was this Mr. Wilkinson?"

"A somewhat horsey-looking young fellow, of perhaps twenty-five years of age," answered the cashier; "clean-shaven, wearing a frock suit and a silk hat. I should certainly not have described him as a gentleman."

"Had he any peculiarity that you can mention; any mark or marks that might lead to his identification?"

Mr. Soames could not remember having noticed any. As a matter of fact, he declared that he was busy at the moment, and believing the signature to be genuine, cashed the cheque without paying much attention to the man who presented it.

"It is a pity for all our sakes that you did not," remarked the inspector drily. "We should in that case have been saved an infinity of trouble. As it is, we have next to nothing to go upon."

The cashier hung his head, and then his face brightened a little and his confidence returned to him.

" There is one thing that I do remember about him, and that is that his left boot heel was worn down on the right side. It isn't very much, but apart from his horsey appearance it is all that I can recall about him. We have so many people passing in and out in the course of the day that it is almost impossible to remember any particular individual."

The inspector made a note in his pocket-book concerning the boot heel, and then turned to his companions.

" I don't think we need trouble the manager any longer, gentlemen," said he. " We have discovered all we want to know."

Having thanked the two gentlemen for their courtesy, they accordingly withdrew. On the pavement outside they paused to discuss the interview which had just terminated.

" That cheque was a forgery, or I'm a Dutchman," exclaimed the inspector. " A marvellously clever forgery, if you like, but none the less a forgery. What beats me is how the fellow Wilkinson managed to get hold of the cheque."

" My experience of criminals has taught me that as often as not they will run the greatest risks in order to throw dust in the eyes of their pursuers," observed the inspector. " However, we must try to lay our hands on Mr. Wilkinson as soon as possible, and to do that I must return without further delay to headquarters. I hope you are not leaving the town, Mr. Tolson. The coroner will be compelled to subpœna you for the inquest, I am afraid."

"And when and where will that take place?"

The other furnished him with the full particulars and then they departed, the police officer returning to the station, and Penfold and Tolson going on to the General Post Office. Here they too separated, Mr. Penfold to return to his office, and Mr. Tolson to enter the building in order to dispatch a telegram. His face was graver even than usual as he bent over the desk and hovered, pencil in hand, above the printed form. "What will he say?" was the question he was asking himself, and it was one that he found it extremely difficult to answer. He did not know that he had ever been called upon to indite a more unsatisfactory wire. At last he made up his mind as to the line of action he intended to pursue, and commenced to write. This was how the message ran :—

Anstruther, Waynflete's Hotel, Strand, London. Come at once. Royal Sussex Hotel, Brighton. Serious news.—TOLSON.

Having dispatched it, he returned to his hotel by cab, calling at the Central Police Station *en route*. Up to that time no news had been received of the missing girl, though the most exhaustive search had been made for her. All sorts of wild rumours were afloat concerning her, and numerous folk had come forward, as is always the case either purporting to be the girl herself or declaring that they had seen her. But in every case their assertions proved to be untrue. The base of the cliffs had been explored, the Downs had been traversed backwards and forwards unsuccessfully, but not a trace of her could anyone discover. Already printed offers of reward had been circulated in every direction, but while they gave certain stimulus to the hunt, they did no real good.

It was with ill-concealed impatience that Mr. Tolson awaited the arrival of the London train by which Eric Anstruther had telegraphed to him that he was travelling to Brighton. However fond as he might be of the young man, he was not altogether looking forward to the meeting. In many cases it is better to be the recipient of bad news than to be called upon to impart them to another. Mr. Tolson felt that it was certainly so in his case—just as Mr. Penfold had done before him. He paced the floor of his sitting-room in deep thought, stopping now and again to look out upon the dull grey sea breaking in sullen thunder upon the shingle. Dusk was falling, and there was every appearance of an approaching storm. It was all in harmony with his own feelings.

At last there was the sound of footsteps in the corridor outside, followed by a tap on the door of his room. In answer to his cry of "Come in," a servant entered to inform him that a gentleman of the name of Anstruther desired to see him. A moment later Eric Anstruther entered the room. In spite of the difference in dress and grooming, he looked but little different to the youth we last saw on the deck of the small steamer in the Caribbean Sea. Even under these altered conditions, he still gave evidence of the same strength, that same lissomness, the same independence, which had characterised him in that far-off land. It would not have been thought from his appearance that he was the possessor of nerves, yet one glance at his face as he greeted the old solicitor was sufficient to show that he was labouring under the weight of a great anxiety, which, do what he would, he could not conceal. He shook hands with Mr. Tolson, and then paused until the waiter had closed the door. Then he spoke.

" For Heaven's sake tell me the meaning of all this," he cried. " What on earth has happened ? Is she ill, or what ? You cannot imagine the agonies I have suffered since I received your wire. I have been imagining all sorts of horrors. Why don't you answer ? "

Mr. Tolson had by this time made up his mind as to his line of action.

" As I told you in my telegram, the matter is most serious," he said. " You know that after mutual consideration we decided that I should bring her here and place her in Miss Pinnifer's charge, hoping by that means, not only to do her good, but to outwit Quintana and his rascally confederates—but, alas ! ' the best laid schemes o' mice an' men gang aft agley.' "

" Oh ! get on, get on," cried the younger man in an agony of impatience. " I don't want to hear you quote Burns. I want to know what has happened. You are driving me to despair by your slowness."

"Have you seen the evening papers?"

"Yes! That is to say, I bought two or three, but I did not read them. I had other and more important things to think of. But what makes you ask the question? What have the evening papers to do with Catalina? Is it hopeless to try and make you explain? Upon my word, Tolson, if you don't soon make a clean breast of what you know, I believe I shall do you a mischief. I am far from being in the humour to be trifled with. Something terrible has happened to the girl I love, and you torment me by not telling me what it is. I thought better of you than that."

"Fair and softly, my dear boy," was the apparently calm rejoinder. "You jump to conclusions too quickly. My object was to break the news to you gradually, in order to prepare you for what is to come. I asked you if you had read the evening papers, because if you had you would have seen that a terrible tragedy has occurred down here to-day. To-morrow it will be all over England."

The young man's voice was hoarse with terror as he put the question, "You are not going to tell me that she has been killed?"

"I pray not," the old man answered, "but she has disappeared no one knows whither. Bad, however, as that may seem to you, it is not the worst. There is more to be told."

" Could anything be worse than that ? Has no attempt been made to find her? Have you done nothing for the daughter of your old friend? Shame upon you, Tolson, shame upon you, I say."

" Your reproaches are unjust," the other answered quietly and without any sign of resentment. " I have done all that mortal man could do. The police are searching for her everywhere; rewards have been offered—what more could be done ? "

" Wait till I take the matter in hand, and you will see. If need be, I will search every inch of ground between Land's End and the North Foreland until I find her."

" But you have not heard me out; there is more to be told."

" I do not wish to hear any more. I have heard enough. What I have to do now is to find my poor lost darling."

" But you *must* hear all I have to tell you. It is the most serious part of the story."

The young man sat down again with an air of resignation.

" Catalina left the house, so it is supposed, between two and three o'clock this morning. About the same time Miss Pinnifer was brutally murdered—her throat was cut from ear to ear."

You might have counted fifty before Anstruther answered. His face was as pale as death, and his hands clasped the arms of his chair so tightly that the veins stood out upon them like thick strings.

" Do you believe it was Catalina who committed the crime? " he asked at last. Then changing his voice—" No, no! forgive me. I can see that you don't."

" But I fear there are others who do," replied Mr. Tolson sadly.

" Then we will disprove it," cried the young man. " Come what may, we will disprove it! And then, by Heaven, I will deal with them ! "

END OF PART II

PART III

CHAPTER X

WHAT good Anstruther thought he was going to accomplish is best known to himself; the fact remains, however, that on leaving Mr. Tolson he made his way to the livery stables of the hotel and hired a saddle horse. If the animal was somewhat more subdued than the bronchos to which he had grown accustomed in South America, it nevertheless served his purpose well enough. On it he rode first to Senlac Square, where he pulled up before Athena House. A small crowd, attracted by the story of the terrible crime, had collected on the pavement and in the roadway, staring at the building which they had probably passed a hundred times before without noticing, as if they could penetrate the mystery of the crime by simply staring at the bricks and mortar. A couple of policemen were on duty, to regulate the traffic as well as they were able. Anstruther beckoned one of them to him, and, bending from his saddle, asked him in a low voice whether anything had been heard of the missing girl. The man shook his head.

" No, sir," he replied; " so far as I know she is still at large, though they are looking for her high and low."

The words " still at large " struck the young man like a blow, for they seemed to hint that this man at least believed Catalina to be guilty. Giving his horse a stir, he rode off at a fast pace in the direction of the Downs, pausing now and again to make enquiries, but always with the same lack of success. The occupants of some of the houses answered him civilly enough, but there were others who asked how many more times they were to be bothered about the matter, declaring that what with the police and other people, they had had no peace all day. Mile after mile he rode on until the darkness showed him plainly that it was useless for him to continue the search.

" Where can she be? " he asked himself as he turned his horse's head homewards. For the first time he began to realise something of the difficulty, one might almost say the impossibility, of the task he had set before him.

It was nearly half-past nine by the time he reached the hotel. Having given up his horse in the yard, he made his way to Mr. Tolson's room. Somewhat to his surprise he found that the lawyer was not alone. Seated at the table in the middle of the room was a short, stout individual, with a clean-shaven, ruddy face and close-cut auburn hair. He looked like a well-to-do farmer of between forty-five and fifty years of age. Before him was spread out a substantial meal, cold beef, bread and cheese, and bottled beer, which he was devouring with great gusto. Mr. Tolson was standing before the fire, his hands under his coat tails and his glasses balanced on the end of his nose.

"Well, my dear Eric," he said, as the young man entered the room, "have you any good news for us?"

"None whatever," the other answered moodily. "I have made enquiries on the Downs, but no one seems to have seen or heard anything of her. If she had vanished into space she could not have disappeared more completely."

As he said this he glanced at the stranger, who was still engaged upon his repast, and who apparently was not taking the least interest in what they were talking about. Anstruther could not help wondering who he could be and why Tolson had mentioned the matter before him. The latter must have seen what was passing in his mind, for he appeared to suddenly recollect himself.

"I beg your pardon, my dear Eric," he said; "I should have made you acquainted with each other before this. Allow me to present to you Mr. Ezra Dexter, of the Criminal Investigation Department of Scotland Yard. He has come down to make enquiries into the case in which we are both so much interested. Mr. Dexter—Mr.

Eric Anstruther, my client and the prospective husband of the young lady who has so mysteriously disappeared.

The detective rose and held out his hand. " Delighted to make your acquaintance, sir," he said, and having shaken hands, promptly re-seated himself and took up his knife and fork, remarking that " it was as prime a bit of beef as he had tasted for many a long day." Of the case itself he made no mention, and doubtless he would not have done so at all had not Anstruther tackled him upon the subject by asking him what his theory was upon the murder.

" I have formed no theory," he answered. " I haven't been in the town an hour and a half yet, and all I know about the case is what I have heard from the inspector and Mr. Tolson here, putting on one side what I have read in the newspapers. As soon as I have finished supper I shall take a run round to the house and make a few enquiries there, so that I may be able to get to work in earnest in the morning. In the meantime I might put a few questions to you that might possibly help to throw some light upon the matter."

" I don't know that I can tell you very much that is likely to be of any use to you," Anstruther replied. " But ask me what you like, and I will do my best to answer you."

" I believe you have known the young lady who has disappeared for some considerable time?" said the other.

Anstruther assented. " He had known her for some time," he declared, and went on to add somewhat irrelevantly " that he was proud of the fact."

" I am glad to hear you say so," said Mr. Dexter politely. " Her father, who was a well-known citizen of the Republic of Colombia, was assassinated, I understand ? "

" That is quite true. He was murdered in the vestibule of the House of Assembly at Bogotá about three months ago. Her mother never really recovered from the shock, and followed him to the grave shortly after."

" And the assassin was never captured ? "

" He had not been when I left the country."

" I am given to understand that the young lady lives in constant terror that she is being followed and that she will share the same fate as her parents; is this so ? "

Anstruther shook his head. " She is in continual dread that she is being followed," he said, " but not by the man who assassinated her father. There was a Spaniard named Quintana who has obtained a great influence over her during the time that her mental balance was somewhat shaken by the troubles she has passed through. He vowed to her that she should never become my wife, and that he would follow her to the end of the world in order to prevent her doing so. She went in continual terror of him, and it was mainly for that reason, and in accordance with the Don's wish, that I brought her home to England."

"Have you any reason for believing that this man followed you to Europe?"

"Unfortunately I have," Anstruther replied. "Though I cannot speak with absolute certainty, yet I feel positive that I saw him three days ago in London. If it was not him it was a man so like him that it must have been his twin brother."

"And where was this?"

"At Waterloo. If it was not Quintana, there is certainly a curious coincidence connected with it, for it was from the Ewell train that I saw him alight."

"And where does the coincidence come in?" enquired the detective. "I am afraid I do not understand."

"Why, Mr. Tolson lives at Ewell, and it is with him that Miss D'Araugo has been staying since her arrival in England. If I were deceived in the likeness, does it not seem strange that this man should have been in that neighbourhood?"

"But could he not have got in at one of the intermediate stations?" asked the other. "However, I grant you that the coincidence is worth considering."

Having finished his supper, Mr. Dexter commenced his preparations for setting off for Senlac Square. It was Anstruther's wish to accompany him, but this the other would not permit.

"I am staying in this hotel," he said, "and if you should not have retired to rest when I return I will look in upon you and tell you if I have discovered anything of importance. I am not very sanguine, however, of doing so to-night."

He took his departure, and Tolson and Anstruther were left alone together. Though they had already discussed the case a hundred times together, they began on it again, speculating as to the reason of the murder, wondering what had become of the unfortunate girl, and hazarding a hundred guesses as to the mysterious Mr. Wilkinson's connection with the matter. So far as they were concerned it was the disappearance of Catalina that weighed most heavily upon them. I am perfectly sure that not for one single instant did either of them connect her in any way with the crime. Tolson believed in her for her father and mother's sake, her lover for her own. The result was the same, though arrived at by two different channels.

" If only we could form some idea as to how she left the house," said Anstruther, as he knocked the ashes out of his pipe into the fireplace. " You say that the maids are quite sure that the front door as well as the back door were both securely locked on the inside when they came down to work this morning?"

" They are positive of it," the lawyer replied. " Miss Tibbits herself locked up on the preceding night, and, from what we have been able to ascertain, they were found in the morning just as she had left them."

" The back door opens into a yard, I understand, while the windows on the ground floor in front overlook a deep area which it would be impossible for her to cross. With every egress barred, therefore, how could she have made her way out of the house?"

"Ah! you have asked me a question which I am totally unable to answer," replied the lawyer. "We must wait and see what Dexter has to say upon the matter. His trained intelligence may be able to accomplish more in an hour than we should do in a week."

Anstruther heaved a heavy sigh; the anxiety under which he was suffering was almost more than he could bear. At last he sprang from his chair, crying as he did so, "I must go for a walk —the house seems to suffocate me. I shall not be gone long, so that if Dexter should return during my absence, keep him, will you? If I don't get some fresh air I believe I shall have a fit."

"Go along then, my dear lad," said the old fellow in a kindly voice, "but don't ask me to accompany you. Just listen to the wind and the rain."

A furious gust struck the house as he spoke.

"And to think that she may be wandering in the dark at this moment," groaned Anstruther. "Oh, Heavens! why did we ever send her down here?"

"Alas, I am as sorry as you are that we did," returned the other. "I would not have had it happen for all I am worth in the world. Poor child! Poor child! However, we must put our trust in Providence and hope and hope that all will come right in the end. Thank God, we are both convinced of her innocence on the question of the murder."

"Yes, we are convinced," growled the younger man. "But are other people likely to be? They do not know her, and, with the usual charity of the world, they would prefer to find her guilty than to think her innocent. Consider what will happen to her if the police get hold of her. Think of the indignities that will be heaped upon her, the gaping crowds, the misery of the prison cell, her portrait in all the illustrated papers, and she, the woman I love and the daughter of Don Miguel D'Araugo. By Heavens! Tolson, it is enough to break a man's heart."

"My dear Eric," said the lawyer, advancing and placing his hand on the young man's shoulder, "you know how deeply I sympathise with you. But do not lose heart; with God's blessing, we will bring her safely through her troubles, and the day will come when you will both look back upon this horrible time as a test for your love for each other, from which you both emerged with honour to yourselves and with a love purified in the Fire of Adversity."

But Anstruther was not in the humour to look at the matter from the other's philosophical standpoint. All he could think of was that poor semiconscious girl in the dark wandering over those pitiless Downs, the storm lashing her with its fury, and she stumbling on and on, unconscious of what she was doing and whither she was going. Unable to bear it any longer he went to his room, donned a hat and mackintosh, and left the hotel.

It was a terrible night. On the front the wind was blowing great guns from the sea, while the rain lashed down as if it were endeavouring to show what it really could do when it set to work in earnest. Anstruther tried to put up his umbrella, but abandoned the attempt as hopeless. The roar of the waves on the shingle was like that of thunder. It was indeed such a day as was destined to be remembered for many a long day to come. But few people were abroad, and such as there were seemed bent on getting to their respective homes with as little delay as possible. Buffeted by the wind, and soaked by the rain, and heedless as to where he was going, Anstruther plodded slowly along. He was fast approaching the Kemp Town end of the town, and to avoid the wind, which seemed to be growing stronger every minute, he turned into a side-street with the idea of finding his way back to his hotel by another route. He had walked perhaps a quarter of a mile when two men caught him up and passed him. Much to his surprise they were talking Spanish, and one of them was telling the other that if he had ever dreamt that the English climate could be so atrocious he would never have left his native land. Anstruther did not hear the other's reply, for a gust of wind howled down the street at the moment and the sound of the second man's voice was drowned by it. He determined to follow them and find out where they were going. Pulling the collar of his mackintosh further over his face, and his cap more over his eyes, so that there might be no reason for their knowing him, Anstruther made his way along the pavement behind them.

The mere fact of his presence in Brighton aroused his suspicion.

What was his business there if it had not to do with Catalina? Here was a nice little problem for him to work out. Keeping thirty or forty yards behind them he watched them turn into another side-street. Just as he reached the corner a fierce gust of wind blew the cap from his head and necessitated a momentary check while he went in search of it. By the time he had recovered it the two men had disappeared. Though he looked on both sides of the street, he could see no sign of them. They could not have had time to have reached the further end, so that it was evident that they must have gone into one of the houses in the vicinity. But which house was it? Being determined not to throw away a chance, he continued his walk, narrowly scrutinising every building as he passed it. Several were plainly uninhabited, the remainder were clearly of the boarding house description. He made his way to the far end of the street, and then crossed the road and returned on the other side. Here his search was equally unsuccessful. The blinds were for the

most part drawn, and, where they were not, no
light showed through. He had begun to despair
of ever locating them, when a room almost opposite
where he was standing was suddenly illuminated,
and, before the blind could be pulled down, he
saw that the man who had lit the gas was none
other than his old enemy, Bartolomé Quintana.
Once more he crossed the road, but this time he
had a definite object in view. He had run his
quarry to ground, and all he had to do now was to
manage by hook or crook to obtain an interview.
What the result of that interview was to be he
did not know. He ascended the steps and rang
the bell, and after a few moments of waiting the
door was opened to him by a small maidservant
of the characteristic third-rate boarding house type.
She had evidently only just come in from her
evening out, for her bedraggled hat was still upon
her head, and she wore a much-patched glove upon
her left hand.

" Would you be good enough to show me to the
sitting-room of the two gentlemen who have just
come in ? " Anstruther asked. " One of them is
an old friend of mine from South America, and I
have only just discovered his address."

The girl regarded him with some suspicion. He
had not mentioned any name, and it was certainly
a late hour for a call. The other guessed what
was passing in her mind, and, realising how
matters stood, placed in her hand two half-crowns.

" It's rather late," she said, " but seeing that

one of them is a friend of yours, I don't see that I can be doing much harm in showing you in. At any rate, I'll chance it. There is only one of them in there just now."

Before Anstruther had time to say anything further she had thrown open a door on the left-hand side of the passage and had announced "A gentleman to see you, sir."

Anstruther entered, to find himself in a fair-sized room, which was furnished with what was plainly the flotsam and jetsam of many sales.

The fire was almost at its last gasp, but standing before it on the hearthrug was the man Anstruther was so anxious to meet. One elbow rested on the mantelpiece, while his left hand was thrust into his trouser pocket. He was better dressed than he had been in America, but otherwise he was just the same. On hearing the maid's announcement, he turned quickly and gave vent to an exclamation of surprise as he recognised the identity of the man before him.

" You ? " he cried. " What in the devil's name brings you here ? Do you know that your life is not worth two minutes' purchase ? "

" It would not be the first time you have tried to take it," Anstruther answered coolly. " I don't, however, think it would be advisable for you to play the same game now. In the first place, this is England—not Colombia, and I fancy you will find it pay you better to keep your animosity until another and more suitable time. What I want to

know is what you have done with the Señorita
Catalina ? ''

There was a look of unaffected astonishment
upon the other's face that was followed by one of
complete bewilderment.

" The Señorita ? '' he repeated. " What do you
mean ? Why do you come to me with such a
question ? You are the man who ought to be able
to give the information, not I ! You brought her
away from her home and you have hidden her
down here.   If I could find out where she is I
would steal her from you, but the worst of it is, I
can't find her.''

If ever there was amazement written on the
human countenance, it was upon Anstruther's at
that moment.   From the first he had believed that
it was Quintana who had had a hand in the murder
of Miss Pinnifer and that it was also he who had
abducted Catalina from Senlac Square.   While he
still saw no reason for departing from that belief,
his instinct told him that there was a peculiar
something in the man's manner that spoke for his
sincerity.

" Do you mean to say ? '' he said, " that you do
not know what has become of her ? Are you lying
to me ? ''

" If we were anywhere but where we are I would
ram those words down your throat, if I killed
you,'' cried Quintana, furiously.

" I am to understand that you swear you know

nothing of her whereabouts?" asked Anstruther again, quite ignoring the other's threat.

"I swear to you that I do not," was the answer. "I know that she is in Brighton, but where she is I have not the very faintest idea. I swear it. Will that convince you?"

"I can't make head nor tail of it," muttered Anstruther. "Why, man, we all believed, the police included, that you had abducted her, if you had not done something worse."

"Have a care, Señor, what you say," cried Quitana, angrily. "By God, I have put up with a good deal, but you must not drive me too far. What do you mean by 'something worse'?"

"Good Heavens, do you mean to tell me that you have not heard of the terrible murder that took place in the early hours of this morning?" asked Anstruther.

"I do not read your English papers. But I heard that there had been something of the sort. An old schoolmistress or something of the kind, was it not?"

"One of the best known schoolmistresses in the town," said Anstruther. "She was found with her throat cut from ear to ear and the Señorita Catalina, whom we placed in her charge, has disappeared."

"And you immediately came to the conclusion that it was I who had murdered the old woman and stolen the girl?" sneered Quintana. "I thank you for your good opinion of me. Fortunately for myself, I am able to prove that a satisfactory alibi. But the girl, where can she be?"

Anstruther groaned.

"We cannot find her," he said gloomily. "Rewards have been offered, and the police have scoured the country in vain."

Quintana began to pace the room with nervous steps. In spite of his bravado he was undoubtedly upset in his mind by the thought that suspicion rested upon him.

"I tell you again and again," he cried with increased vehemence, "that I know nothing whatsoever of the matter. I caught a glimpse of her in London with that old notary and discovered that she had left for Brighton. I followed, but have neither seen nor heard of her since my arrival in the town. Señor, you must help me in this matter. Whatever happens they must not arrest me."

"And why not?"

"Because I am the only one who can find her," he answered.

"And how do you propose to account for the fact that you are following her about the world in this fashion when you know that she is the betrothed wife of another?"

"All is fair in love and war, my dear Señor Anstruther," he replied, with an attempt at jocularity. "I loved her before you did and I love her still. Ask yourself, if our positions were reversed, would you be content to sit still and see her stolen from you by another man? No, of course you would not. You would fight to the bitter end to win her, and that is exactly what I am doing, and what is more, what I intend to go on doing. For the present, however, I am willing to sink all rivalry and to assist you in the search for her."

This was more than Anstruther could stand.

" Allow me to assure you," he said, " that we have not the least desire for your assistance. It was without doubt her fear of you that drove her from the house, and we shall never find her so long as she believes that you are pursuing her."

" You take a very high-handed tone, Señor. If I were not able to make allowances for your present anxiety, I should resent it."

" Whether you resent it or not is immaterial to me," remarked his rival coolly. " But for your own sake I should advise you to be careful how you act. The mere fact that she continually confessed her fear to other people that she was being followed by someone from South America would be sufficient to justify the police in keeping an eye on you."

" But I am innocent of any connection with the affair at all," he answered stoutly enough, though the colour of his face rather belied the bravery of his words.

" That may be," said the Englishman, " but they would ask you to prove it. If you take my advice you will return to South America as quickly as possible. At present England is not a healthy place for you."

"You want me to go away and leave her to you, I suppose," was his rejoinder. "I thank you, no. I shall stay and see this thing through, whatever is the consequence."

Anstruther's only answer was to leave the room; and this he did so quickly as almost to upset Quintana's compatriot, who had been standing with his ear to the keyhole in order that he might not lose a word of the conversation that was going on inside. Putting on his cap, he opened the front door and let himself into the street, but before he walked away he made a careful note of the number of the house, in case it should be necessary to visit it again. Then he strode on through the storm in the direction of his hotel.

His heart was as heavy as lead as he made his way along the rain-washed pavement. Had Quintana told him the truth when he said that he knew nothing of Catalina's whereabouts in Brighton, or was it only another card in the game he was playing? Taking into consideration all he knew of him, he was aware that he could not trust him. To gain his own ends he would deceive his own friend without a moment's compunction. He was without heart, without honesty and without remorse.

"I fancy, however, the knowledge that the police have an eye upon him will make him careful as to his actions, even though they have not a shadow of justification for believing that he had a hand in the actual murder of the unfortunate Miss Pinnifer."

On reaching his hotel, Anstruther made his way to the sitting-room which he and Mr. Tolson shared. It was in total darkness.

" The gentleman had gone to bed," said a waiter who chanced to be passing at that moment. " He told me to tell you when you came in."

Burning with impatience though he was to communicate his intelligence to his friend, the other realised that he must wait until the morning to unburthen himself.

CHAPTER XI

" My dear lad," said old Mr. Tolson next morning when they met at breakfast, " you must excuse me for not having sat up for you last night. But to tell you the honest truth, I was so sleepy and so worn out with all I had gone through during the day that I verily believe I could not have stayed up another hour had my life depended on it. You are not angry with me, I trust ? "

" Why should I be ? " asked Anstruther. " I can quite understand that you were tired. It is not often in one's life, thank goodness, that one is called upon to cram so much into a single day. And now, while we breakfast, I will tell you what I did last night. I think you will agree with me that it is not without interest."

He then proceeded to describe his adventures from the time that he left the hotel until he returned to it again. He told him of his meeting with Quintana and of the interview that had taken place

in the sitting room. When he referred to the
assurance the Spaniard had given him to the effect
that he was quite ignorant of the whereabouts of
Catalina, a puzzled expression made its appearance
on the old lawyer's face.

"Are you prepared to believe that the fellow
was telling you the truth," he enquired, with what
sounded very like a note of sarcasm in his voice.
"For, if you are, I certainly am not. Remember
the poor girl's cry in the night: "I am being
followed—I am being followed." Now if it was
not Quintana whom she believed to be in pursuit
of her, who was it? Answer me that. According
to your account, he admits having seen her in my
company in London. Was that merely a matter
of accident? Of course it was not. One's
common sense tells one that. He must have
followed us and thus have discovered that we had
departed for Brighton. Confirmation is given to
this suggestion by the fact that he is here now.
The whole thing is as plain as doomsday. I
wonder that a clear-headed young fellow like you
can be so easily taken in."

Anstruther felt more than a little nettled by the
other's remark, nevertheless he kept it to himself.

"I admit the London episode," he said, "and
also the fact that he is now in Brighton. But I
honestly do not believe that he knew of her connection with Miss Pinnifer and Athena House. If
he did, all I can say is that his behaviour last

night was one of the most marvellous pieces of acting I have ever witnessed in my life.''

'' I have not the least doubt in the world about that,'' was Mr. Tolson's rejoinder, as he decapitated an egg with the air of a professional headsman. '' He made up his mind from the first to take you in, and, egad, it looks very much as if he had succeeded.''

'' You don't pay a very high compliment to my intelligence,'' growled Anstruther, who found that his temper was fast getting the better of him. '' However, I suppose that time will show us who is right and who is wrong. In the meantime, what are we to do? Every hour is taking her further and further away from us. Good Heavens, Tolson, if this goes on much longer, I believe I shall be driven mad. I am haunted by the most dreadful fears for her safety. One moment I picture her found dead among the rocks at the foot of some terrible cliffs; the next I see her wandering like some poor mad creature on the country side, or floating far out at sea with the waves breaking over her, her hair all dank and sodden like that of a woman whose body I once helped to bring ashore in Rio Harbour. And to think that this should be the fate of the girl who was the apple of her father's eye, the sunbeam of his house, and the most envied and courted maid in all the length and breadth of Colombia.   Oh! the bitter irony of Fate! ''

Tolson, who had finished his breakfast and had

risen from the table, went round and placed his hand upon the young man's shoulder.

"My poor boy," he said, in a kindlier tone than he had yet used, "do not think that I cannot realise how great your trouble is. But, please God, there are happier days in store for you. The Great Providence which watches over us all will restore her to you, and in the days to come you will look back upon this time as a black page in your life's history that only served to throw into relief the happier pages that went before and followed after it. But who is this?"

As he spoke there was a knock at the door, and in response to his cry "Come in," Mr. Dexter from Scotland Yard made his appearance.

"Good morning, gentlemen," he began. "If you will allow me I will take off my coat. The weather is milder this morning and I almost wish I had not brought it with me."

"Have you breakfasted?" asked Mr. Tolson, standing before the fire with his hands thrust deep down into his pockets. "If not, let me ring and tell them to bring you up something."

But it appeared that the other had made his morning meal and that all he stood in need of now was a cigarette which he took and lighted. A long clay churchwarden would have been more in keeping with his personal appearance, but as he was wont to tell people, he did not smoke only for enjoyment, but rather because it tended to sociability.

"May one be permitted to ask the result of the

enquiries you made last night? " asked Mr. Tolson when the detective had blown out the match and thrown it into the fireplace.

" There cannot be the least harm in the world in telling you," replied the other, " particularly as I have not managed to discover anything. I went to the house as I told you I should do and was received by the two amiable ladies whom you have described to me. They corroborated what I already knew, throwing in a few conjectures of their own which were about as useless as such ideas usually are. The elder lady is convinced that the crime is the work of the assassin who murdered Miss D'Araugo's father; Miss Tibbits, however, holds to the belief that the young lady herself should be held responsible for it. Both failed entirely to account for the fact of the doors being locked and chained on the inside, which to my thinking is the most extraordinary part of the whole extraordinary business. How the young lady managed to leave the house is, I must confess, an infathomable mystery. Unless she possessed an accomplice, which it is quite certain she did not, the doors could not have been shut to, the key turned in the lock, or the chains put up. I have gone into the matter from every point of view, and the more I think it over the less able I am to understand it. I have had some puzzling cases pass through my hands in my time, but I can safely say that I have never known one that looked so simple at first and became so complicated later. There is the young lady theory for instance—"

"You are not going to say that you believe her to be guilty?" cried Anstruther quickly. "For pity's sake don't say that."

"I am not going to say it, and for the simple reason that I have nothing to base any suspicion upon. It is true that she has disappeared in a very strange fashion, but you could find a dozen reasons to account for that. She might have been an unconscious witness of the crime. Indeed the murder itself might have been the result of an attempt to carry her off. The schoolmistress might have heard a noise and have gone to her pupil's assistance, and so have met her fate. That would in a measure account for the blood-stains on the floor near the latter's door. The assassin, whoever he may have been, must have picked the murdered woman up and carried her back to her own room, laid her upon the bed, and then have escaped from the house, taking Miss D'Araugo with him. But there again you are confronted with this question, how did they get out of the house and lock the doors behind them? That is the pivot upon which all the rest turns."

"Might he not have had a confederate in the house among the servants?" asked Mr. Tolson.

"It is possible of course, but I do not think probable," the detective replied. "I have questioned the maids and, so far as I can judge, they all appear to be highly respectable women, such as one would expect to find in an establishment of that class."

"And the resident governesses?" asked Anstruther. "What about them?"

"They may be dismissed from the question at once," responded Dexter. "No, if we want to get at the bottom of the mystery, we must look in some direction which we have not yet thought of. There is the man, for instance, of whom you spoke to me last night, the Spaniard named Quintana, who you say followed you from America. We must do our best to find him and discover what his movements were on the night in question."

"I have already found him," answered Anstruther, with not a little exultation.

"The deuce you have! And where is he?"

The other furnished him with the address and then went on to describe the interview he had had with him and the deductions he had drawn from it. Once or twice during his narrative he could not help glancing at Mr. Tolson, for he knew that the latter was still labouring under the impression that he had been hoodwinked by the astute Spaniard. What was worse, Mr. Dexter seemed to entertain the same view.

"I must have a watch placed over Mr. Quintana's movements," said the gentleman from Scotland Yard. "It would never do to allow him to slip through our fingers."

"Do you really think he is connected with it?" asked Anstruther.

" It is too early to venture an opinion," replied the other quietly. " He is either innocent, or he is playing one of the biggest games of bluff I have ever met with in my professional career. We have still to settle which it is. I shall make it my business this morning to take a look at the house in which he is staying. I don't suppose for a moment that he would hide her there, but there is always the chance that he took her there prior to despatching her somewhere else. Will you be good enough, Mr. Anstruther, ' to give me as detailed a description of the individual in question as you can. I only hope that your appearance on the scene last night has not induced him to pack up his traps and clear out. After your telling him, if not in so many words, at least by imputation, that he is being watched by the police, it will surprise me very much if he does not develop a desire to put as many miles as possible between himself and them within the next twenty-four hours."

For the first time Anstruther began to regret the impetuosity which had induced him to enter the other's house on the preceding night. It would have been far better had he merely located him and then have given the information to Dexter to be dealt with as that worthy might deem most advisable. But still, the thing was done and could not be undone, and there was nothing for it but to hope for the best.

" May I ask what your programme is for to-day? " enquired Mr. Tolson.

" I shall make my way first to the address which Mr. Anstruther has given me," the other replied. " After I have made some enquiries there I shall proceed to Senlac Square and continue my investigations. Then there is the inquest at half-past two, which I shall be compelled to attend, as also I presume, both you gentlemen will be."

" Would you have any objection to my accompanying you to Senlac Square ? " asked Anstruther. " I would endeavour not to get in your way."

" You are quite welcome to come if you wish to," said the detective, rising from his chair as he spoke. " Though I fear you will not find it very interesting."

" Anything connected with this miserable affair must perforce be interesting to me," remarked the younger man. " I want to see the room which was occupied by my poor sweetheart, and I should also like to have an opportunity of putting a few questions to the governesses."

" Very well, sir, if you will be near the house at eleven o'clock, I will meet you there and take you in with me. It is not my custom to have anyone with me when I am working up a case, but in this instance I am prepared to make an exception in your favour."

Anstruther helped him on with his coat, and then the other bade them good-bye, warning the younger man not to be late for his appointment.

" That is a most remarkable man," said Mr.

Tolson, when Dexter had left the room. "He has unravelled some wonderfully entangled skeins in his time, though you would not think so from his commonplace appearance and unsophisticated manner. It was he who brought that notorious criminal Barridge to the docks and eventually to the gallows. He boarded for three months with that iniquitous family the Colenburghs, who committed murder on a wholesale plan in a street at the back of the Tottenham Court Road. If he had given them the least clue as to his identity he would have shared the fate of their unfortunate victims. But they did not suspect him, and as a result, he was enabled to bring them all to justice and to secure for them the fate they so richly deserved. On one occasion he acted for my firm in a most intricate and dangerous matter, and it was then that I first made his acquaintance."

Anstruther gazed at him in astonishment.

"I was not aware that you had ever met before," he said. "He did not appear to recognise you yesterday."

"That is exactly his way," remarked the lawyer. "He never knows anyone after his business with them is completed. And when you come to think it over, I fancy you will admit that it is a very good rule. If he were to be on terms of intimacy with all the folk with whom he has been brought in contact during his professional career, he would scarcely be able to call his life his own. When

this case is finished, in all probability he would not
know you if he met you in the street.''

''You mean that he would pretend that he did
not know me?'' said Anstruther sharply.

''Well, it amounts to the same thing in the
end,'' replied Mr. Tolson. ''Every time I am
brought in contact with Dexter the more I admire
his sterling qualities. He has the tenacity of the
bull-dog mingled with the sharpness of the terrier.
His apparent stolidness is alone sufficient to put
his quarry off their guard. They little guess how
actively his brain is working behind that placid
forehead.''

''Do you mean then, that you think he knows
more in this present case than he gives us to
understand?'' asked Anstruther.

But the other only replied that he was not com-
petent to form an opinion on the subject.

Half-an-hour later the younger man, who in the
meantime had received a subpœna to attend the
inquest that afternoon, stepped into a cab and
ordered the man to drive him to Senlac Square.
When he had dismissed the vehicle he walked
along the pavement in the direction of Athena
House. A crowd which had hung about the place
all the previous day was as large and curious as
ever. It still wanted a quarter of an hour of the
time of his appointment with Dexter, so, for want
of something better to do, he mixed with the
throng and listened to the opinions of those who

professed to be in a position to solve the mystery of the crime once and for all.

"What is the use of telling me that sort of tale?" demanded an old gentleman in a shabby frock coat and a silk hat that had seen better days. "The whole thing is as plain as the nose upon your face. The whole thing is a plant from beginning to end. What's this foreign girl that the police can't find? Why, she's just what you might call a confederate."

"What's a confederate?" asked somebody standing near.

"Go on, silly," laughed a woman in a shawl, who from her manner should have been the enquirer's wife, "haven't you ever heard of a confederate? Why, he's the chap at the conjuring shows that sits down with the awjience and helps him to gammon the public."

"But what's that got to do with this here murder?" asked the other, who had not been best pleased at being called a silly before the crowd.

"What I say is," continued the old gentleman in the frock coat, "that this here foreign girl was a confederate put into the house to find out where the money and vallables was and to let in the gang when they came to take 'em. The old woman wakes up and gets her throat cut for her pains. Then the whole lot of them clears off with the swag. You mark my words, that is the way it will all come out in the end."

Having said his say he looked round him to note the effect his address had produced on his immediate neighbourhood. Some evidently agreed with him, while others had theories of their own which they were quite ready, nay even anxious, to propound. To Anstruther's sorrowful dismay he very soon discovered that, whatever theories might be advanced as to the actual committal of the murder, the consensus of opinion was that the unfortunate Catalina was, if not the actual perpetrator, at least an accessory to the crime. The one and apparently universal wish was that she might speedily be captured and brought to justice.

" Good heavens, what fiends they are," muttered Anstruther to himself as he overheard a delicately-featured woman observe to a companion, " it's a pity they can't find her and let her loose on the town ; it wouldn't be my fault if I didn't write the Ten Commandments on her face with my nails— the murdering cat."

Unable to bear any more of this sort of talk, he left the crowd and strolled down the Square in search of Dexter. It was time for him to put in an appearance, but as a matter of fact he did not do so until nearly half an hour later.

" Your amiable friend Mr. Quintana has given us the slip after all," he observed when they had greeted each other. " He and his companion left their lodgings early this morning and, so far, I have been unable to obtain any clue as to their present whereabouts."

"That is bad news," returned Anstruther. "I am afraid it is all my fault. I should not have attempted to see him last night. I suppose you did not make any discovery of importance?"

"Well, that all depends upon how you look at it," returned Dexter, throwing what remained of his cigarette into a puddle. "But I have learnt enough to convince me that, whatever else he may have had a hand in, he was not present at the time of the murder. On the night in question he did not leave the house at all. The landlady's husband is prepared to swear to this, for he saw them go to bed a little before midnight, and he slept with the key of the front door under his pillow. He passed a restless night and, had they gone out, or attempted to do so, he must inevitably have heard them. No, I think we may as well dismiss Quintana from this portion of the case once and for all. That he intended to steal the girl there can be little or no doubt—in fact I understand he said as much to you, but I have quite made up my mind that he did not do so from Athena House."

"It seems to me that the case is getting more and more complicated every hour," Anstruther continued with a sigh. "If Quintana had no hand in the murder, who had? If he did not take Miss D'Araugo from the school, who did? If there was no confederate in the house to put up the chains and turn the keys after her, who did the work?"

Mr. Dexter shook his head.

"I warned you that it was an intricate case,"

he said. "You are able now to judge for yourself."

Anstruther was suddenly struck by an idea. With so many other things to think of, he had temporarily lost sight of one character in this momentous drama.

"What about Wilkinson?" he enquired. "The man who paid in Mr. Tolson's cheque at the Bank to Miss Pinnifer's credit and who at the same time cashed a draft for two hundred pounds in his own favour. It seems to me that the whole affair resolves itself into the answer to these three questions—When, where, and how, did he obtain possession of those cheques? It has been proved that Miss Pinnifer saw no one, that is to say, no stranger of the opposite sex. It is also quite certain that she could not have drawn it after she had been killed. What is more, the bank authorities are, as you know, decidedly of opinion that the cheque drawn in favour of bearer is a forgery. Surely this all seems to point to the conclusion that Mr. Wilkinson, whoever he may be, is the man to whom we should look for an explanation."

All through this long speech delivered as they walked along the pavement towards Athena House, Mr. Dexter had been nodding his head like a toy Chinese Mandarin.

"They are searching for Mr. Wilkinson now," he said quietly, and then lapsed into silence until they reached the house.

After a few moments' conversation with the

sergeant of police on duty, they ascended the steps and entered the house. It was with a strange feeling that Anstruther crossed the threshold. His spirits were low enough already and the silence of the house with the horrors that lay upstairs forced them to an even lower level. He began almost to wish that he had not agreed to accompany the detective, but, after a struggle with himself, he put the thought away as being suggestive of the failure to do his duty towards Catalina. The sombre, cheerless hall, with its massive furniture was in half darkness, as were the stairs leading to the corridors above. As they were divesting themselves of their great-coats, a small cadaverous lady with cork-screw curls and a black cap made her appearance from a room at the further end of the passage. She evidently recognised Dexter, for they shook hands, after which she glanced at Anstruther as if wondering who he might be. Mr. Dexter interpreted the look and immediately made them known to each other. Then it was that the young man remembered that this was the lady who so resolutely maintained the belief that it was Catalina who was guilty of the murder of her mistress. From that moment he took an instinctive dislike to her, which, however unjust it may have been, was scarcely to be wondered at under the circumstances.

"We will now get to work," said the police officer. "There is a good deal to be done and very little time in which to do it. I want to have

o

my facts as far as possible before me in time for the inquest. We need not trouble you further, I think, Miss Tibbits," he continued, as he observed that the little lady was preparing to· accompany them on their tour of the house. " I already have the geography of the building at my fingers' ends."

" That is of course for you to say, sir," remarked Miss Tibbits. " If you should desire my help in any way, I am quite at your service. There is, alas, little enough for us to do just now."

As she said this she glared at Anstruther as if she were prepared at a moment's notice to hold him responsible for the calamity which had made such a change in her life. The look, however, was lost upon the young fellow, who was staring at the door of Miss Pinnifer's study as if he half expected that lady to make her appearance from it.

Having obtained the key from the officer on duty in the house, Dexter led the way to the room in question and when Anstruther had entered, closed the door carefully behind them. Bidding the latter sit down, he himself set to work upon an exhaustive examination of the apartment and its contents. The window, he had already satisfied himself, looked out over the area and, unless he had been provided with a ladder, it would have been practically impossible for the perpetrator of the crime to have made his exit by that means. He examined the floor, which was already beginning to be coated with dust, opened the drawers

in the escritoire and centre table, and carefully
scrutinised the contents of each.

"No trace of Mr. Wilkinson there," was his
invariable comment as he pushed drawer after
drawer back into its place. "But where is her
cheque-book and where is her paying-in book?
Perhaps, Mr. Anstruther, you would not mind
asking Miss Tibbits to be good enough to come
to me here. It is possible she may be able to put
us upon the right track."

Only too glad to escape from the room if only
for a few moments, Anstruther willingly did as he
was asked. He had the good fortune to find the
lady in question crossing the hall as he emerged.
She accompanied him to the study, but declared,
in answer to the questions put to her, that she had
not the least idea where the deceased lady was in
the habit of keeping any of the books used in
connection with her banking account.

"But in the course of your long association with
her," said the detective in his usual placid manner,
"you must surely have seen her write cheques?"

"Cheques without number," was the reply.
"Nevertheless I do not know where she was in the
habit of keeping the books. I always presumed
that it was in one of the drawers of the writing-
table. Are you quite sure that you have searched
thoroughly, sir?"

Mr. Dexter smiled indulgently.

"I have turned every drawer inside out," he
replied, "but without success. It is very strange

that it should not be here—seeing that within a few hours of her death she must have drawn a cheque in favour of a certain Mr. Wilkinson. By the way, do you happen ever to have met that gentleman?"

Miss Tibbits considered for a few moments before she replied. At last she appeared to make up her mind.

" No," she said firmly and with conviction, " I am quite sure that I have never met him. Indeed, I do not remember Miss Pinnifer ever having mentioned his name to me."

" He did not call here the day before yesterday? Be good enough to think well before you answer."

" No, I am quite sure he did not," was her reply. " The rate collector called during the morning to leave demand notices, and Mr. Tolson later. Two ladies visited Miss Pinnifer during the afternoon to arrange about sending their daughters as pupils, and Herr Strudmeyer had an interview with her before he left in order to report on the progress of a pupil who was leaving shortly for Germany to take up seriously the study of the violin. Those were the only people from the outside who saw my late employer during the day."

" Many thanks for your lucid explanation," responded Mr. Dexter. " I do not think we need trouble you any further, Miss Tibbits, at least not at present."

The lady withdrew, and the detective sat back

in his chair and gave himself up to the contempla-
tion of a richly-engraved signet ring which he
wore on the little finger of his left hand.   His
reverie must have lasted for nearly five minutes,
during which time Anstruther sat listening to the
monotonous ticking of the clock upon the marble
mantelpiece, and asking himself again and again
what could have become of the girl who was more
to him than life itself. This agonising suspense
was driving him mad, and yet he seemed powerless
to do anything to help matters. The mere fact
of the inquest that afternoon lay like an intolerable
weight upon his shoulders.   What if the jury
should come to the conclusion that she was guilty
of the murder and gave a verdict to that effect?
The blood in his veins turned to ice at the very
thought of such a thing.

" Well," said Mr. Dexter, rising to his feet,
"there is nothing more to be discovered here.
Let us turn our attention to the rest of the house."

They did so, passing from room to room with
the exception of the death chamber, until they
reached the topmost storey, which was unused,
save for one room in which were stored the trunks
and boxes of the pupils that had not as yet been
forwarded to them.

" For all we have discovered as yet, our morning
has been comparatively wasted," said Anstruther,
petulantly, as they descended the stairs once more
to the hall.

Possibly Mr. Dexter was revolving some problem in his mind, for he offered no reply to his companion's speech. Indeed, he did not open his lips until they had left the house and were almost at the end of the Square. Then he said, more to himself than to his companion,

" When we find Mr. Wilkinson, I fancy we shall all be more than a little surprised."

CHAPTER XII

PUNCTUALLY at two o'clock that afternoon, the coroner opened the enquiry as to the circumstances under which the famous schoolmistress, Miss Pinnifer, came by her death. It is needless to say that the court was crowded to suffocation, for after all, human nature is but human nature, and sad though it may be to say so, a latent love of the morbid is to be found in almost every breast. Having briefly explained to the jury the reason of their being summoned to attend at the court, they were sworn, and, escorted by the coroner, departed to view the body. Mr. Tolson and Anstruther occupied seats in the forepart of the court with Mr. Dexter near at hand. The detective, by long usage, had become inured to such affairs, but to the two gentlemen, the prospect it afforded fell little short of a nightmare. The crowd at the back of the court were discussing the case in all its bearings but, fortunately for him, Anstruther did not hear them. He would indeed have been a brave man who would have stood up before them at that moment and have declared that Catalina was not guilty. The all-knowing public would have laughed him to scorn.

At last, and after what appeared a period of interminable waiting, the coroner and jury returned to the court. It was evident from their faces that some of the latter had not even yet recovered from the horror of the visit they had just paid. The coroner took his seat and the case commenced.

Having described the main outline of the affair, so far as it was known, he went on to speak of the respect in which the deceased lady had been held by all who had known her. She was an old inhabitant of the town, and her Seminary for Young Ladies was the model of what such an establishment should be. That she should have been so foully and brutally murdered, for the medical evidence would point conclusively to the fact that murder it could only have been, was a blot upon their fair fame as a town, as well as a menace to the safety of law abiding citizens. There was some applause at the back of the court on hearing this, but it was instantly suppressed. Having wound up his remarks with the assertion that he was sure they would do all that lay in their power to assist in unravelling the mystery and bringing the guilty to justice, he gave orders that the first witness should be called. This proved to be the doctor who had been summoned to the house by the English governess. He deposed to having been called to Athena House, Senlac Square, on the morning in question. He was conducted to the bedroom of the deceased, where he made a careful examination of the body. Life was already extinct. When asked how long he considered it was since death had occurred, he declared that to the best of his belief, it had taken place from six to seven hours before he was called to the house. The wound, which was a very severe one, had been inflicted by an extremely sharp instrument, in all probability by a razor. He was firmly of opinion that it was not a case of suicide. He then went into details which were as unintelligible to Anstruther as they were to the greater number of those present. When he sat down he was followed by the inspector of police, who gave a description of what he had found when he was summoned to the house. He had known the deceased lady for many years, and had always entertained a great respect for her. He had made enquiries of the governesses in the house, had examined the various rooms and exits, and had communicated with the authorities at Scotland Yard. He had never seen the missing pupil, and was not able in any way to account for her mysterious disappearance. Rewards had been offered for any information that might lead to her discovery, the police throughout the country had been notified, but so far no trace of her had been discovered. In answer to a question addressed to

him by a juryman, he declared that he had been
informed that she was somewhat eccentric, the
result of a severe mental shock she had received in
South America some months before. Mr. Ben-
fold, the lawyer, was next called, and corroborated
what the inspector had already said. He had acted
as Miss Pinnifer's legal adviser for upwards of
thirty years, and he was quite sure that she was the
last person in the world to have taken her own
life. He had seen her only two days prior to the
terrible event, and had found her in the best of
health and spirits. He knew nothing of the
circumstances connected with the arrival of the new
pupil, nor had he seen that young lady. When
he sat down his place was taken by Miss Tibbits.
Her tall, angular figure, draped in a mantle which
had once been the property of the deceased lady,
presented a singular appearance. Her face was
deathly pale, but her thin lips were as firm set as
if she knew her duty to Society, and was going to
do it at any cost to herself. With perfect self-
possession she described the events of that terrible
night, beginning with the moment when she had
been wakened from sleep by the screams of the
new pupil, and had accompanied Miss Pinnifer to
the latter's room, and ending with the terrifying
discovery she had made when she had entered her
principal's bedchamber some hours later. She
had been in Miss Pinnifer's service for twenty
years, and was quite sure that her employer would
never have attempted her own life. On being

asked whether she had been present when the new pupil arrived, she replied that she had been summoned to Miss Pinnifer's private room almost immediately. In reply to further questions, she went on to give her opinion of the unfortunate young lady. There could not be the least doubt, she declared, that the other's mind was unhinged —a statement which was borne out by her singular behaviour in the middle of the night. Miss Tibbits had had several hundreds of young ladies under her care, but never one who had behaved in such a fashion as this young South American lady. When asked if she had any theory to account for the other's disappearance, she shook her head, as if to suggest that she knew more if she only cared to tell it. In reply to a juryman she stated that she was quite at a loss to account for the manner in which she had left the house. She was quite sure that the doors and windows had been securely fastened, and that they had been found to be in the same state on the morning following. She also was perfectly sure that Miss Pinnifer had no enemies, for a kinder and better-hearted lady never walked the earth.

Miss Tuckett, the English governess, was next called. In a dry, matter-of-fact voice she described how Miss Tibbits had informed her of the catastrophe and how she had immediately gone off to summon the police, the doctor, and Mr. Penfold, the lawyer. Like so many others, she had been awakened in the middle of the night by the screams of the new pupil, but she had heard nothing else till she had met Miss Tibbits later on. Together they had visited Miss D'Araugo's apartment, and had found it empty. She, like her colleague, knew no one who would have been likely to perpetrate such a terrible crime, nor could she give any reason why the new pupil should have departed so mysteriously.

When she had resumed her seat Mr. Tolson's name was called and he was sworn. He described the circumstances under which he had placed Miss D'Araugo, the daughter of a much-respected Colombian old friend, in Miss Pinnifer's charge. The unfortunate young lady had within the last six months passed through a great deal of trouble, which had brought about a species of melancholia, which was not to be wondered at when all the circumstances of the case were taken into consideration. Her father had been assassinated, her mother had died shortly afterwards, and she herself had been compelled to fly from her own country in order to escape from a certain person who had acquired a very sinister influence upon her. He had placed her with Miss Pinnifer because he thought the discipline of the school and the companionship of other young members of her sex might under judicious management exercise a beneficial effect upon her. Until lately she had been a high-spirited, warm-hearted girl, a popular favourite, famous as much for her beauty as for her great wealth. That she would take the life

of a harmless and amiable lady like Miss Pinnifer
was too absurd to be seriously considered. She was
both morally and physically incapable of such a
deed. When asked to account for her disappearance on this particular night, he had to confess
that he was unable to do so. The only theory he
could put forward was the fact that she lived in a
continual fear that she was being followed by the
man whom she had left her own country to escape.
This fear she had expressed in the nightmare that
had so alarmed the household. Was it not feasible
that, under the influence of that fear, she had left
the house to hide herself elsewhere? How she
had made her exit he could not say, but nothing
would ever convince him that she knew ought of
the terrible crime that was the subject of this
enquiry.

"Call Eric Anstruther," said the coroner, after
he had made some notes. The young man in
question immediately rose and went forward. He
stated that he was an Englishman, and that he had
spent some years in the Republic of Colombia.
He had been employed by Don Miguel D'Araugo,
and was betrothed to the latter's daughter. After
the assassination of her father and the death of
her mother she was in a very despondent condition,
which was aggravated by the persistent attentions
of a certain individual who was anxious to induce
her to marry him. So persistent had these
attentions become, and so bad was the effect they
produced upon her, that no course was left him

but to remove her from the country. He therefore brought her to England and placed her with her guardian, Mr. Tolson, who was also his own solicitor. After mature deliberation she was brought to Brighton and to Athena House, where it was hoped, for a time at least, her troubles would be at an end. The statements which had been made to the effect that her mind was unhinged were quite erroneous. Her mind was as evenly balanced as it had ever been. The doctors had declared that all she required to restore her to her previous condition of robust health was complete change of scene and thought. The latter they thought might be accomplished by the companionship of young members of her own sex. All this went to endorse what the previous witness had said, namely, that she was quite incapable of having committed the vile deed which some people seemed so anxious to attribute to her. There was something about the way Anstruther made this confident assertion that aroused the sympathy of a large number of those present. The young man's handsome face and confident bearing had a good deal to do with this. As one old woman was heard to remark, " He be a proper sort of young man to stand up for his sweetheart whether she scragged the old woman or not."

This expression seemed to echo the sentiments of her audience, though it had no effect on the actual court itself. When a number of minor witnesses had given their evidence, including the bank cashier who had cashed the cheque drawn by Miss Pinnifer in Mr. Wilkinson's favour, the coroner addressed the jury. He recapitulated the various circumstances connected with the case, and at last despatched them from the court to consider their verdict. During their absence, Anstruther could scarcely control his impatience. The excited whispering of the crowd behind him stretched his already overstrung nerves to breaking pitch. Catalina's good name, nay, her very life perhaps, depended on the next-few minutes, and the public was deriving enjoyment from the suspense. Presently the jury returned and took their places as before. A sudden hush fell upon the court, and everyone leaned forward eagerly as if anxious not to miss a word. Anstruther clenched his teeth and waited. For the first time he became aware that the foreman of the jury was a little man with a mole on his left cheek. That mole aggravated him, though he could not have told you why. Then he became aware that the Coroner was addressing them, asking them what verdict they had arrived at. The foreman made some reply, but Anstruther's heart was beating so wildly that he could not hear what was said.

" What is it? What is it? " he whispered to Mr. Tolson. " Why can't the man speak louder? "

" The verdict is one of wilful murder against some person or persons unknown, and the jury express a hope that the police authorities will do their utmost to discover the whereabouts of the young lady and of the mysterious Mr. Wilkinson. All things being considered, it is better than I had hoped for. One never knows what an English juryman will do till he has done it."

"In this case, however, he has acted very pleasantly," said Anstruther. And then to himself he muttered, "My poor little girl. Thank Heaven they have found out as to your guilt."

When they had passed into the street once more they were joined by the inspector of police and Mr. Dexter.

"Well, Mr. Tolson, what do you think now?" asked the former.

"So far as the verdict is concerned I am pleased," replied the old lawyer. "But I am still at as much of a loss as before to understand what it all means. When you come to review the evidence it is plain that we have learnt nothing new. What do you think, Mr. Dexter?"

"At the present time I am trying not to think," answered that astute officer. "Like Mr. Micawber, I am waiting for something to turn up."

"Can't you turn it up?" asked Anstruther, almost irritably. What he considered to be the dilatoriness worried him more than he could say.

"No," said the detective, "just for the present it must be our rôle to possess our souls in patience with the hope that the other side will make a move and thus give us the clue we want. In the meantime, a constant search will be kept up for the missing young lady, and also for the mysterious Mr. Wilkinson. When that gentleman is discovered I fancy we shall be able to see a gleam of daylight ahead."

" And who is looking for him, may I ask? "

The detective smiled indulgently.

" My dear sir," he said, " it would take you a long time to count the number of people who are on the watch for him. The only surprise I feel is that he has not been discovered before this."

" Well, he can't be found too soon for my liking," Anstruther replied. " This anxiety is driving me nearly crazy."

" Never fear, my dear sir," said the inspector. " We will do our best for you. As Mr. Dexter says, it cannot be very long before Mr. Wilkinson's whereabouts are discovered. He will then be called upon to explain how those two cheques came into his possession, and it is more than likely then that his answer to the question will help us materially to solve the mystery connected with Miss Pinnifer's murder. You must not be too down-hearted, sir. As the old saying goes, ' It is a long lane that has no turning,' and the smallest circumstance may be sufficient to put us on the right track."

Confident though his words were, they did not tend very much towards raising Anstruther's drooping spirits. It was in vain that Mr. Tolson argued with him; he refused to be comforted. When he retired to rest that night he was about

as miserable a specimen of a young Englishman
as could have been found in a long day's march.
For nearly two hours he lay upon his bed brooding
over his troubles, and this may possibly be held
accountable for the nightmare which took possession of him as soon as he fell asleep. It was such
a dream as he had never experienced in his life
before—so vivid, so real, that even now he cannot
recall it without a shudder. It seemed to him that
he was wandering in the dark over a vast land, the
sky was overcast with clouds, and at intervals
heavy gusts of wind hurled themselves upon him
as if to sweep him from the face of the earth.
Without being conscious of where he was going,
he struggled on, until, and just as he was giving
up all hope of finding shelter, he saw before him a
blurred outline of a large and lofty house. Not a
light showed from the windows, nor was there any
sound, save the howling of the wind round the
corner of the building. What had once been the
enclosing walls was now only a mass of fallen
stone, the gate had long since been deported, and
his feet told him that the drive was now but little
better than a bed of weeds. He approached the
front door and tried the handle. It turned, and
he entered. His footsteps on the bare boards of
the hall roused the echoes of the deserted house.
He had nothing on him wherewith to make a light,
nor would the draught which assailed him from
every side have allowed one to live, had he

possessed the necessary materials. Just as he was wondering what he should do next, a great shriek rang out. It was a woman's voice and his instinct told him that the person who had given utterance to it was Catalina. But where was she? Again the shriek rang out, and he endeavoured to locate it, but in vain. Raising his own voice he shouted that it was he, Eric Anstruther, and that he had come to save her! He implored her to call to him again in order that he might be able to locate her whereabouts. But no answer rewarded him. Again he called and with the same result. He groped his way down the hall until he found the staircase, which he began to climb. At length he reached the landing. By this time his feet were heavier than lead, and yet all the while he knew that she must be near at hand if only he could find her. Again the cry rang out, "Save me, Eric! Save me!" He hastened forward, only to find himself falling—falling through space. Before he reached the bottom of that terrible abyss he woke to find himself sitting up in bed—the sweat of pure undiluted terror rolling down his face. Sleep being out of the question, he lit his candle and read until it was time to get up.

How he got through that day and the following night, I don't think he could tell you himself. He went to bed in fear and trembling lest he should be visited with another attack of the nightmare which had produced such an effect upon him on the previous night. This may possibly have been the reason why he was destined to go through it all again. Once more he saw the dreary, wind-swept stretch of land—once more he approached the deserted house, entered it and heard the piteous cries of help from the woman he loved and, as on the previous occasion, he fell headlong into the abyss before he could come to her assistance.

As before, he woke in an agony of terror, and again he read his book until it was time for him to rise and dress.

" If this goes on," he said to himself, as, hair-brushes in hand, he contemplated his haggard face in the glass, " I shall pretty soon be as bad as any hysterical schoolgirl."

Even a cold bath failed to rouse him.

When he descended to their sitting-room for breakfast, he found that Mr. Tolson was already there. A letter in an unknown handwriting lay upon his plate. He opened it without interest. His apathy was immediately dispelled when he saw that it was from Dexter. It was short and to the point and ran as follows :—

> Scotland Yard,
> 25th October, 19—.
>
> DEAR Mr. ANSTRUTHER,
> We have at last located Mr. Wilkinson. All being well, I shall interview him soon after you receive this and communicate

the result to you as soon as I am in a position to do so.

Yours obediently,

EZRA DEXTER.

"Thank goodness, Wilkinson at least is found," said Mr. Tolson, and Anstruther echoed the sentiment.

CHAPTER XIII

WHATEVER else he may or may not have been, Bartolomé Quintana was far from lacking in energy or resource. When he set himself to do a thing he usually did it, and unhappy indeed would be the lot of the man who should have the audacity to come between him and his project. He had made up his mind that Catalina should be his wife, and the mere fact that she had always disliked him had not the slightest effect upon him. The knowledge that it was Anstruther who was his rival added fuel to his determination. He had hated him from the moment that he first saw him, and the remembrance that so far he had been out-witted by the Englishman was indescribably bitter to him. That Catalina had disappeared was, so he argued, a point in his favour, always provided that his enemy did not become aware of her hiding-place before he himself was cognisant of it. The question to be decided was where *could* she be hiding. He was, moreover, fully conversant with Dexter's movements, and had also informed himself that the other had gone to Town in search of the mysterious Mr. Wilkinson. Leaving his companion to watch affairs in Brighton, he, in his turn, set off for the metropolis. That the man who had cashed Miss Pinnifer's cheque and had paid in that carrying Mr. Tolson's endorsement was playing some part in the affair, he felt perfectly convinced in his own mind. He accordingly packed his bag and departed, travelling, strangely enough, by the same train as that which conveyed Anstruther to the Great City. As Fate would have it, neither was aware that they were fellow passengers, or it is more than probable that this story would have had another and an even more extraordinary ending.

On reaching Town, Anstruther drove to his hotel and then to a certain small yet famous tavern in the neighbourhood of Fleet Street. There he found Mr. Dexter waiting for him, looking more like a prosperous farmer than ever.

"You have not wasted much time, sir," he said, as they shook hands.

"I am much too anxious to do that," the other answered. "Are you sure that it is safe for us to talk here?"

"Perfectly safe," the detective replied and forthwith led the way to one of the boxes at the further end of the room. Refreshment was ordered for the good of the house and instructions were given to the elderly waiter to take good care that they were not disturbed.

"Now what have you to tell me?" asked Anstruther. "You have arrested Winkinson, I suppose?"

To his surprise, the police officer shook his head.

"No," he said, "it is not time for that yet. It is necessary that we should watch him a little longer. He is not the only one in the business, and we want to find out who the others are. But you need not be afraid, sir, we have him under observation and he will not escape us."

"Nevertheless, I should feel happier if he were safely under lock and key. This anxiety is making an old man of me."

"Ah, you are thinking about the young lady," put in the detective.

"And you of Miss Pinnifer's murderer!"

"No!" Dexter retorted. "I don't know that I was thinking more of one than of the other. You mark my words, sir, when we have it all worked out you will be more surprised than you dream of at present."

"What do you mean?"

"That is just what I can't tell you at present. When I am at work on a job like this, I never like to say anything until I am quite certain of my facts. But there is one thing I am quite positive of, and that is, that the young lady is as innocent as I am of the murder."

"God bless you for that assurance!" cried Anstruther, grasping his companion's hand and shaking it warmly. "I suppose I must wait in patience for you to tell me more?"

"I am afraid you must. But be sure that I will not keep you waiting any longer than I can help.

I suppose, sir, you have not seen or heard anything
more of that South American individual, Quintana?"

Anstruther replied in the negative. All he
knew was that the other had vacated his Brighton
lodgings and had disappeared no one knew
whither.

"Well, we shall find him when we want him,"
Dexter answered, confidently, and then rose to bid
Anstruther "good-bye," but not before he had
promised to communicate with him at his hotel
should he have anything of importance to relate.

Why he should have done so, he could not have
said, but the fact remains that the young man felt
distinctly happier as his cab carried him along
westward. That Dexter would not buoy him up
with false hopes he felt certain, and, if he had not
said so in so many words, he had at least given
him a hint that he was on the track of the real
murderer, and that he would be able in course of
time to prove Catalina's complete innocence.

That evening he returned to Brighton.

While he had been busy, Quintana on his side
had not been idle. Quite by chance he had happened upon Dexter within half an hour of the
latter bidding farewell to Anstruther and what was
still better, without the latter being aware of the
fact. He had followed him; had seen him meet
a tall, austere individual, without a doubt a brother
detective, and had waited in the vicinity until he
had seen them part company, whereupon he
permitted Dexter to go while he shadowed his

double. His instinct was not at fault. He had not waited half an half before he saw that something or someone had attracted his man's attention. Though he had never seen him before, his natural astuteness told him that the newcomer was no less a person than Mr. Wilkinson, the man whom he was so anxious to meet. He was a tall, cadaverous youth, who looked more like a bookmaker's clerk than anything else. There was a shifty expression on his face, and more than once he threw nervous glances over his shoulder as if he were afraid he was being followed. Though he was not aware of it, this was exactly what was taking place. The procession was rather a curious one—first Mr. Wilkinson, the collar of his great-coat turned up about his ears, his hat cocked rakishly on one side, and the bottoms of his trousers turned up over boots which had evidently seen better days. Following him at a distance of perhaps fifty yards, came the detective, and some yards behind him, on the opposite side of the street, Señor Quintana, lynx-eyed and with the stamp of a foreigner plainly imprinted upon him. They made their way along the Strand, turned down Northumberland Avenue, and thence by way of the Embankment, Citywards once more. Darkness had fallen long since and Quintana was beginning to find the pangs of hunger intruding themselves upon him by the time they reached the minor street in which they had originally picked up their quarry. Here Mr. Wilkinson disappeared, and for upwards of half an hour Quintana waited for him to emerge again.

He did not do so, however, and then it was that
Quintana decided on a bold stroke.   He waited
until he had seen the detective relieved before
putting it into execution, after which he crossed
the street and boldly approached the house which
he had seen the other enter.   It was of the ordinary
minor boarding-house description and stood badly
in need of repair.   He rang the bell and, when it
was answered, enquired whether he could see the
gentleman who had just come in.   The curl-
papered damsel who had opened the door to him
suggested that he probably meant Mr. Walker,
" who had to do with racehorses," and invited him
to follow her, which he hastened to do.   He found
Mr. Walker-Wilkinson in a small apartment which
served the double purpose of a bedchamber and
sitting-room.   He was smoking a short clay pipe
and held a railway time-table in his hand.   This
fact alone struck Señor Quintana as being signifi-
cant.   " Something has made him nervous," he
thought to himself, and his instinct told him that
if he did not want to lose his man, he must act at
once.

" Mr. Walker, I believe," he said, by way of
introduction.

Mr. Walker eyed him with evident disquiet.

" That's as may be," he said.   " What is your
business with me ?   I don't know that I have ever
seen you before."

" And probably when I have told you my business you will say that you never want to again,"
observed the Spaniard.   " I am here to do you a

good turn, if possible.   You left Brighton in rather a hurry."

Mr. Walker's face, on hearing this, was worth going a good many miles to see. His conscience told him that he was discovered, and he neither knew what to say or do. He decided, however, to try a bold stroke.

"I don't know what you mean," he said. "I was never in Brighton in my life."

"Then I suppose you don't know Senlac Square, or any of the ladies connected with Miss Pinnifer's establishment? You were never inside the bank when you cashed a cheque for two hundred pounds, endorsed by the lady who had the misfortune to be so cruelly murdered the other day? It won't do, Mr. Walker-Wilkinson, or Wilkinson-Walker, whichever you prefer to call yourself. There are people who are prepared to swear to you."

For a moment he thought the unfortunate young man was about to have a fit, but at last he managed to pull himself together.

"If you say that I killed the old lady, you are lying," he said, tremblingly. "I never laid a finger on her."

"You will have to prove that?" answered the remorseless Spaniard. "And I fancy it will take you all your time to do it."

The wretched youth's pluck had entirely deserted him. He sat down at the table and covered his face with his hands.

"What are you going to do with me?" he

asked, quite believing that his emissary hailed from Scotland Yard and would escort him at once to the nearest lock-up.

"That depends upon how you answer the questions which I am going to put to you," said the other. "Tell me the truth and it is just possible that I may find it in my heart to give you a chance—but lie to me, and nothing under the sun can save you."

"But what can I tell you?"

"Tell me where that young girl is—the Señorita D'Araugo?"

"I know nothing about her," he answered. "I have never seen her."

Here Quintana lost his temper altogether.

"Very good," he said. "As you won't take advantage of the opportunity I have given you, you can't blame me if you find yourself with a rope round your neck."

"But I swear I know nothing about it," moaned the young man, who by this time was almost too terrified to speak. "So far as I know, I have never set eyes on her, and even if I had I should not have touched her. It isn't likely."

"Then how did you become possessed of those two cheques?"

"They were given me," he answered, doggedly.

"And who gave them to you?"

But he refused to speak. It was not until Quintana had pressed him for some time and was almost giving him up in despair, that he condescended to answer. When he did, it was to implore his persecutor to give him until the morning, when he would make a full and free confession of all he knew about the matter.

Realising that he was powerless to extract any information from him, if he did not intend to tell, the Spaniard agreed to his proposal, taking care, however, to let his victim understand that he would be watched in the interval, and that if he attempted to make his escape, he would be immediately arrested.

"You will find me right enough when you come," said the other. "It would be no use of my thinking of running away. I have no money and nowhere to go—if I had any."

Quintana looked at him with an expression of real scorn upon his face.

"What a poor, half-hearted chicken it is, to be sure," he said to himself, and then, after a final warning, he prepared to take his departure. He had not been as successful as he could have wished, but, on the other hand, he had not failed altogether.

When he reached the street once more it was to find the detective still at his post of observation. He, in his turn, entered a small eating house exactly opposite, and seating himself at a small table in the window, ordered a meal and the evening paper. He had disposed of the first and was digesting the news contained in the second, when what he had expected happened. The door of the house he had lately quitted opened, and a man came out. In spite of the disguise he had assumed, Quintana experienced no difficulty in recognising him. He immediately paid for his meal and passed into the street. The chase that followed was a long one, but eventually Quintana found himself on the platform of Victoria Station awaiting the departure of the Brighton Express. Having made sure that Mr. Wilkinson had taken has seat, he too embarked, and was presently on his way back to London-by-the-Sea. For the sake of the game he was playing with so much earnestness, it was a pity that he did not know that a telegram had already been despatched to Eric Anstruther by Mr. Dexter, informing him of the departure of the two men and stating his intention of following himself by the next train.

" Now what does this mean ? " asked Anstruther as he handed the message to Mr. Tolson.

" It looks as if matters are approaching a crisis," replied the old gentleman. " I presume you will be at the station to meet them ? The telegram, I notice, does not say whether they are travelling together or whether they are spying on each other."

" I will be able to tell you that when I return," observed the younger man. " Now I am going to see what I can do to alter my appearance. Whatever happens, I must not allow them to become suspicious. To do that at this critical stage of the proceedings would be worse than fatal."

" And is there nothing that I can do to help ? " enquired Mr. Tolson. " It does not seem to strike you that I am as anxious as you are to penetrate the mystery."

"I am going to ask you to remain here until Dexter makes his appearance. By that time it will not be my fault if I do not know something about what is going on."

"Good luck go with you, my dear lad. Never fear, we will find the sweet maid yet."

Then Anstruther went off to prepare for his adventure.

CHAPTER XIV

So great was Anstruther's impatience, that he reached the railway station nearly a quarter of an hour before the express was due. By way of a disguise he wore a soft felt hat, the broad brim of which half covered his face, and a heavy ulster whose collar, when turned up, hid his mouth and luxuriant moustache. In order that the chance of detection should be still further lessened, he made use of a pair of dark spectacles, carried a stout umbrella and still stouter hand-bag. Thus equipped it would have taken a sharp pair of eyes to distinguish in this burly, almost Teutonic traveller, the spruce young man who had journeyed to and from London that day. As I have already said, he arrived at the station a considerable time before the train made its appearance. In order not to attract the attention of anyone, who might be on the lookout, he kept as far as possible to the darker portions of the platform, whence, from behind his blue glasses, he carefully scrutinised everyone who approached him. At last the train was signalled and, amid the shouts of porters and the clatter of brakes, pulled up at the platform. Acting on a plan he had arranged beforehand, our amateur detective made his way quickly to the foremost luggage van as if he were in search of articles of his own, in the meantime he kept a close watch upon the various passengers as they passed him. He had not long to wait before his patience was rewarded. Well wrapt up against the chilliness of the evening, Quintana came along the platform and passed Anstruther without recognising him. That he was watching for some one was easily seen, and Anstruther found no difficulty in guessing the identity of the second party. He let them pass and then, in his turn, joined the procession. With Mr. Wilkinson leading the way, Quintana some distance behind him and Anstruther bringing up the rear, they passed out of the station. The youngest man called a cab and, having given some address to the driver, entered it. As soon as he had departed, the Spaniard called up another vehicle and set off in pursuit, whereupon Anstruther prepared to do the same.

"Do you see that cab?" he said to his man, who gruffly intimated that he did. "Then drive after it, but whatever you do, don't allow it to get out of sight or to imagine that we are following. I wonder where on earth they can be going," he said to himself, as his Jehu whipped up his horse.

" One thing is as certain, however, as the nose upon my face, and that is, they are not in league with each other."

Through street after street the three vehicles rattled on their way, until it seemed to the impatient young man as if the journey would never come to an end. The excitement of the chase had taken full possession of him, but he wished that Dexter had been with him to bring the weight of his experience to bear upon the solution of the problem, the solving of which meant so much to him. He was still thinking of this when his cab man opened the shutter in the roof. " They've both stopped, governor. One outside the ' pub ' yonder, and the other at the corner of the street."

" Well, drive past them and pull into the first side street you come to."

The man did so, and when he had alighted Anstruther liberally rewarded him and dismissed him. He could see that the other would willingly have questioned him, but he had no intenton of allowing him to do so.

Leaving the side street, he passed quickly into the main thoroughfare, so quickly, indeed, that he came within an ace of colliding with Mr. Wilkinson himself, who was hurrying along, his umbrella held low down to protect him from the pouring rain. On the other side of the way was another pedestrian, Quintana without a doubt.

" Why don't you look where you are going ? " growled Wilkinson, with an oath. " You might have bowled me over."

Anstruther apologised, and then turned to his left hand as if to continue his walk in that direction. He did not go very far, however, before he stopped and looked round. The two figures were still hastening along, as if both were anxious to get to their destination with as little delay as possible.

Once more he took up the pursuit, and with renewed eagerness. It surely could not be long now before the mission of one of them at least would become apparent. On reaching the end of the street, which consisted almost entirely of second-class boarding-houses, their leader turned sharply to the right, passed down another and meaner thoroughfare and then disappeared from view with an abruptness that was as disconcerting to one, at least, of his followers as it was unexpected. A moment later Quintana also vanished, but this time Anstruther was close enough behind him to see that he had disappeared into a narrow lane which, at first glance, resembled a *cul-de-sac*. In reality it communicated with, or perhaps it would be better to say that it formed part of, an extensive right of way into which opened the tradesmen's entrances of a number of large houses. It was lighted by one solitary lamp, whose wind-tossed flame revealed no trace of a human being.

"Well, I am sure Quintana at least turned in here," remarked Anstruther to himself. "But, if so, where is he now and what on earth part of the town am I in?"

But as he was quite unable to answer this to his

satisfaction, he contented himself with examining
the various doors in the hope that they might
elucidate the mystery. Their numbers, however,
did not tend to enlighten him. He discovered that
they were twenty-four in number, or in other words
twelve on either side of the lane. There were
lights in some of the houses, but with the exception
of the roll of wheels in adjacent streets, the steady
downpour of the rain and his own footsteps on the
stones, all was as silent as the grave. Fearing that
the start he had allowed them might have enabled
them to pass through the alley and out at the other
end, he hurried on, only once more to come into
collision with a pedestrian, in the shape of a policeman. The officer's suspicions were aroused when
he become cognisant of the strange appearance of
his assailant. He took in the slouch hat, the
coloured glasses, and more particularly the hand-
bag, with a comprehensive glance.

"Now look here," he said, "what I want to
know is, your business in there. You have been
up to no good, it's my opinion, and as soon as I
have seen the sergeant, I'll have to take you along
to the station."

"But this is absurd," cried Anstruther angrily.
"You are exceeding your duty and, if you detain
me, I shall report you to the authorities. I was
following two friends of mine, and they gave me
the slip in that alley."

"A likely tale," continued the officer. "I have
been here for the last few minutes and, if your
friends had come through, I should have seen

them. No, it won't do. Just hand over that bag
and come along with me."

Anstruther ground his teeth with rage. If the
man persisted in conducting him to the police
station, his evening's work would be useless, and
yet, angry as he was, he could not help seeing how
appearances were against him. The more he
tried to explain, the more suspicious the man
became. At last, and just as he was giving up all
hope, assistance came and from a most unlikely
quarter. They had proceeded some fifty yards or
so down the street, and Anstruther was in a condition bordering on lunacy, when, who should
approach them but a mackintosh-clad figure with
a walk that the young man could have distin-
guished from a hundred.

" My goodness, Dexter," he cried, " you could
not have made your appearance at a better moment.
This man believes me to be a suspicious character,
and was in the act of taking me to the lock-up.
Tell him who I am, there's a good fellow."

Dexter told him—at the same time revealing his
own identity. The policeman, to whom the famous
detective's name was a household word, was
covered with confusion and apologies. He had
received special instructions to watch the lane in
question and to ascertain the business of any
suspicious character he might see hanging about
it. The handsome tip he received for doing his
duty placed matters on an eminently satisfactory
footing.

" Now, for goodness' sake tell me where we

are?" enquired Anstruther. "And how you come to be here?"

"Both are easily answered. I came down by the same train as the other two. Owing to a mistake on the part of a man who was to have met me at the station, I was delayed for nearly three minutes and, in consequence, the only vehicle I could procure was one with a slow horse and the stupidest driver I have ever had the ill-fortune to meet. Of course he lost sight of you, but I had my suspicions of the direction in which the others were proceeding, and came on here as quickly as possible."

"But you haven't told us yet where ' here ' is," replied Anstruther.

"Why, Senlac Square, to be sure. This lane runs at the back of Athena House. Steady, sir, steady, what's the matter?"

The other could scarcely speak for excitement.

"Then they've gone in there," he cried. "They've gone in there. They gave me the slip, but I know that they entered the lane and, if the constable says they did not come out at this end, well, it's evident that they must have entered one of the houses. I ask you which it would be likely to be?"

The detective's answer might have meant anything. It consisted of the simple word "Ah!" A moment later he continued, "It is very evident that, by hook or crook, we must gain admission to the house, if only for the sake of the women who are in it. Those two rascals don't mean any good, you may be sure."

" But why should they want to visit the house ?
If you ask my opinion, Wilkinson committed
burglary, even if he didn't go as far as murder.
There may be some clue of which he is anxious to
remove the traces."

" But what about Quintana ? How do you
account for his accompanying him ? "

" I am perfectly sure that he is not accompanying him. My firm conviction is that he is
following him because he believes that the other
knows more than a little concerning Miss
D'Araugo's disappearance. Don't you think I
am right ? "

" It is certainly an ingenious theory," was
Dexter's reply. " Now we have got to see how we
are going to get into the house. Every moment is
of importance."

He called up the constable and questioned him.
The man admitted that in byegone days he had
more than once partaken of the cook's hospitality
at the house in question, but, since the murder, the
only domestic employed was a charwoman who,
to use his own expression, was as cranky an old
woman as ever stepped in shoe leather.

" Well, let us go down the lane and take a look
at the place," observed Dexter. " We may be
able to judge then what is best to be done."

The back door of the famous Seminary for
Young Ladies presented no remarkable appearance. It was plainly, but solidly constructed, and
appeared to be bolted as well as locked. On the
right and left of it were windows, all securely

barred. The outlook was distinctly unpromising.

"Do you think, sir, if I was to give you a leg up, you could manage to get over the wall and drop into the garden?" asked the constable of Dexter.

"It is just possible I might," replied that gentleman, "but it won't be a pleasant operation. Those bottle ends require consideration. However, if you are prepared to make the attempt, Mr. Anstruther, I am also willing to do so."

"Let me go first," said the younger man. "I'll thrown my ulster over the top and then lend a hand to haul you up."

Five minutes later they were in the garden—such as it was, and were tiptoeing across it towards the window of the schoolroom in which Mr. Penfold had acquainted Mr. Tolson with the news of Miss Pinnifer's murder and of his ward's disappearance. This was also shuttered and fastened.

"Ah, we must try somewhere else," observed Dexter, without any sign of disappointment.

His companion, on the other hand, was nearly beside himself with impatience. They moved along the side of the house, carefully examining the various windows, but still without success. At last they reached one which gave evidence of being somewhat frailer than its companions.

"We must force it, whatever happens," remarked Dexter, and commenced to pull with all his strength at the bars, Anstruther helping him. The wood-work was rotten with age and neglect, and one by one they yielded to the force brought to bear upon them. When sufficient had been removed to allow them to creep through, the old-fashioned catch was pushed back with the aid of a knife, and the window itself pushed up. On entering they found themselves in a small lobby, which had doubtless once been used by the pupils as a hanging place for their hats and coats.

" Be careful how you tread," whispered Dexter, when he had removed his boots and his companion had followed his example.

A faint light was burning in the hall from which the lobby opened. There was also a light in the drawing-room, the door of which was ajar, as also was that of the deceased lady's study on the opposite side of the passage. The two men had reached the foot of the stairs and had just concealed themselves in the shadow when the sound of a woman's voice speaking with uncontrollable passion reached their ears.

" Good Heavens, it is Miss Tibbits," Dexter heard his companion mutter.

He was right. It was certainly that lady who was speaking, but who was it she was addressing. Was it Wilkinson or Quintana?

" You will ruin me before you have done," she was saying. " Do you think I have not suffered enough? You have taken all I have in the world and there is nothing left for me but a life of poverty, while you are wasting my hard-earned savings on race-courses and in billiard-rooms. I will do no more for you."

It was Mr. Wilkinson who made answer.

" You had better drop that rubbish," he said,

brutally. "I tell you I must have a hundred pounds to-night, happen what may."

"Then you will not get it from me," was the uncompromising retort.

"Won't I? We will see about that. How would you like it if I was to go to the police and tell them about that Spanish girl, eh? That would not suit your book, you know. They might even think you had had a hand in the murder of the old gal."

Quivering with excitement, Anstruther was about to spring to his feet and enter the room, but Dexter seized him with a grip of iron and pinned him down.

"Wait, wait," he whispered, "and watch."

He had scarcely spoken when the door of the murdered woman's study was opened, and Quintana crept softly out. He crossed the hall and approached the room opposite. Taking a revolver from his pocket, he entered boldly.

"I have heard enough," he said. "You are my prisoners. As for you, young man, I warned you this afternoon that if you attempted to leave London you would be arrested. You have only yourself to blame. You will both be charged with the murder of Miss Pinnifer."

The last word had scarcely left his lips before a snarling sound like that of a wild beast reached the ears of the listeners outside, followed by an exclamation in Spanish, and the noise of a fierce struggle, and then a pistol shot, and Quintana's voice called out "I am shot."

Dexter and Anstruther sprang to their feet and rushed into the room. It was a strange and terrible sight that met their eyes. Crouched in one of the further corners, his cadaverous face convulsed with terror, was the wretched young man who had called himself by the name of Wilkinson, while on the floor in the centre of the room, in a litter of broken glass and china, lay Quintana, a large pool of blood already forming beside him. He had been shot through the lungs, and was already *in extremis*. Kneeling beside him, with a face more like that of a hyena than that of a human being, was Miss Tibbits. Her hair had fallen in wild disorder about her shoulders, and in her hand she held a still smoking revolver, which she must have wrested with superhuman force from the other. She seemed unconscious of their entry and was chattering incoherently to herself. It was only necessary to look at her face to see that, however sane she had been before, she was now a raving mad-woman. Instinctively both men fell back from her in loathing.

" I call you both to witness that she shot me," muttered Quintana. Those were his last words. He was dead.

Almost immediately the unfortunate woman became coherent.

" I killed him," she cried, " and I would kill him again, because he would have taken my son—the prettiest boy that ever you set eyes on—but a forger, gentlemen. He made me steal Miss Pinnifer's money, and he copied her signature so beautifully that it would have made you laugh to see it. She found me out and I killed her, and that Spanish girl saw me do it, so I drugged her and hid her in the box-room to starve. It used to cool my brain to go up and listen at the door to hear her groans. Now where's my boy—my pretty boy?"

Here she fell to talking nonsense once more, but Anstruther did not stop to hear it. He had seized and lighted a candle, and was flying upstairs as if for dear life. The situation of the room in question was well known to him, and one blow of his shoulder burst the locked door open. Holding the candle aloft, he looked about him; the boxes of the pupils had not yet been removed, but were ranged one upon the other against the further wall. To his astonishment, there was no one in the room, nor was there any other door save that by which he had entered. His heart sank within him. It looked as if the mad-woman's statement was an hallucination after all. He had turned away and was about to leave the apartment when his quick ears caught the sound of a low moan. In less time than it takes to tell, he had crossed the room and was tearing the wall of boxes down. Yes! there was a door there, and by some strange chance, the key had been left in the lock.

"Catalina, my darling," he cried, "I am coming to save you."

He threw open the door and entered, and piteous indeed was the sight that met his gaze. Catalina, the high-spirited Catalina, lay bound upon the floor. In the candle light she looked more dead

than alive.   Her lovely face was only a shadow of
her former self, and she was quite unconscious.
With the knife that he had used to force the
window-catch downstairs, he cut the bonds that
bound her and carried her down to a room on the
next floor, where he placed her on a bed and went
off in search of Dexter, who he found handing over
his prisoners to the police.   Him he begged to go
in search of the nearest doctor, and also to send
a messenger to fetch Mr. Tolson.   The latter's joy
on finding that his ward had been discovered, I
must leave you to imagine for yourself.   To all
intents and purposes, my story is finished.

*   *   *   *   *   *   *

Catalina and Anstruther were married three
months ago, and are now wintering in the South of
France.   Two years have elapsed since that
terrible time in Brighton and, though she has quite
recovered her health and beauty, she is never likely
to forget the terrible experience through which she
passed.

Mr. Tolson, who saw them a fortnight ago, tells
me that they talk of returning to Colombia for a
short stay next year, but I have my doubts about
it.   As for the other characters of my story, I saw
Mr. Dexter's name the other day figuring in
connection with a notorious case, the tangled skeins
of which he had unravelled with his customary

skill. Miss Tibbits, who, it appeared, was a married woman when she entered Miss Pinnifer's service, died hopelessly insane in a criminal lunatic asylum, while her son, who confessed to the forgery of the murdered woman's name, is, I believe, still working out his sentence in one of our large convict establishments.

THE END

LEICESTER.

IN TUNE ● ● ●

WITH THE INFINITE

OR

*FULLNESS OF PEACE, POWER
AND PLENTY*

BY

RALPH WALDO TRINE

*Within yourself lies the cause of whatever enters into
your life.   To come into the full realization of your
own awakened interior powers, is to be able to condition your life in exact accord with what you would
have it.*

CONTENTS

LONDON: GEORGE BELL & SONS

PORTUGAL STREET, LINCOLN'S INN

1905

105th Thousand.   *Attractively Bound*

IN TUNE WITH THE INFINITE

or

Fullness of Peace, Power, and Plenty

By RALPH WALDO TRINE

Price 3/6 *net.*   *Postage* 3d.

✷

PAGE 145.

What one lives in his invisible, thought world he is continually actualizing in his visible, material world. If he would have any conditions different in the latter he must make the necessary changes in the former. A clear realization of this great fact would bring success to thousands of men and women who all about us are in the depths of despair. It would bring health, abounding health and strength to thousands now diseased and suffering. It would bring peace and joy to thousands now unhappy and ill at ease. . . .

PAGE 180.

When apparent adversity comes, be not cast down by it, but make the best of it, and always look forward for better things, for conditions more prosperous. To hold yourself in this attitude of mind is to set into operation subtle, silent, irresistible forces that sooner or later will actualize in material form that which is to-day merely an idea. But ideas have occult power, and ideas, when rightly planted and rightly tended, are the seeds that actualize material conditions. ✲ ✲ ✲

PAGE 144.

Thoughts of strength both build strength from within and attract it from without. Thoughts of weakness actualize weakness from within and attract it from without. Courage begets strength, fear begets weakness. And so courage begets success, fear begets failure. . . .

PAGE 50.

The only thing that any drug or any medicine can do is to remove obstructions, that the life forces may have simply a better chance to do their work. *The real healing process must*

be performed by the operation of the life forces within. . . .
There are almost countless numbers to-day, weak and suffering
in body, who would become strong and healthy if they would
only give God an opportunity to do His work. To such I
would say, *Don't shut out the Divine inflow.* Do anything else
rather than this. Open yourselves to it; invite it. In the
degree that you open yourselves to it, its inflowing tide will
course through your bodies a force so vital that the old obstructions that are dominating them to-day will be driven out before
it. . . .

PAGE 72.

Fear and worry and all kindred mental states are too expensive for any person, man, woman, or child, to entertain or
indulge in. Fear paralyzes healthy action, worry corrodes and
pulls down the organism, and will finally tear it to pieces.
Nothing is to be gained by it, but everything to be lost : . . .

EXTRACTS FROM LETTERS

I cannot withold any longer the joy and peace that is mine since
reading " In Tune with the Infinite." It has given me more inspiration, more joy, more peace, more love, and more of everything that is
good than any book that I have ever read, and when I say this I do
not except even the Bible.—A. S. F.

I know of nothing in the entire range of literature more calculated to
inspire the young than the " Life Books," and to renew the life of the
soul in young and old.—C. L.

Nothing I have ever read so lifts my soul up to the Divine, so
amazes me, creating new and better thoughts, greater aspirations and
a determination to live up to its teachings. It is so grand, so elevating,
yet so plain.—Mrs J. A. J.

It is absolutely the most interesting book I have ever read, and I
shall read it again and again.—O. R. P.

That book will carry blessings to multitudes. I congratulate the
author on putting so profound a theme in so simple a way that the
common people can get it.—Rev. W. H. M.

Every page gives me solid food. I want all my friends to take it
and read it. but I cannot yet spare it. I must re-read it again and
again, for it is such a help to my life.—Mrs J. T. H.

It appears to me not merely strikingly apt in its counsels and pre-
cepts, but also a brilliant contribution to our literature. The style is
clear and concise, and the teachings embodied in it are far more
practical than those of any similar book it has been my good fortune to
peruse. . . . I am sincerely grateful for the inestimable benefit it has
been to me.—(Marquise) C. L.

OTHER BOOKS

BY

RALPH WALDO TRINE

Crown 8vo, 3s. 6d. net. Postage 3d.

WHAT ALL THE WORLD'S A-SEEKING

35th Thousand in England and America

Small 8vo, 1s. each net. Postage 1½d.

THE GREATEST THING EVER KNOWN

37th Thousand

The moment we fully and vitally realise *who and what we are*, we then begin to build our own world even as God builds His.—*From Title-page.*

. . . It unfolds the secret of our underlying strength, and shows what it is that gives us power to fulfil the real and living purposes of our being.

EVERY LIVING CREATURE

19th Thousand

The tender and humane passion in the human heart is too precious a quality to allow it to be hardened or effaced by practices such as we so often indulge in.—*From Title-page.*

An eloquent appeal and an able argument for justice and mercy to our dumb fellow-creatures. A good book for those whose characters are being formed, and for all who love justice and right.

CHARACTER-BUILDING : THOUGHT POWER

30th Thousand

A thought, good or evil, an act, in time a habit, so runs life's law ; what you live in your thought world, that, sooner or later, you will find objectified in your life.—*From Title-page.*

In "Character-Building : Thought Power," Mr Trine demonstrates the power of mental habits, and shows how by daily effort we may train ourselves into right ways of thinking and acting. His teachings are sound, practical, and of priceless worth.

LIFE AND LIGHT BOOKS

Prettily Bound, 1s. net each. Postage 1½d.

The Greatest Thing Ever Known. By RALPH WALDO TRINE, author of "In Tune with the Infinite. *37th Thousand.*

Character - Building: Thought Power. By RALPH WALDO TRINE. *30th Thousand.*

Every Living Creature; or, Heart-Training through the Animal World. By RALPH.WALDO TRINE. *19th Thousand.*

Fate Mastered—Destiny Fulfilled. By W. J. COL-VILLE, author of "The World's Fair Text-book of Mental Therapeutics."

Marcus Aurelius Antoninus. G. LONG'S Translation.

Epictetus Discourses. G. LONG'S Translation. *2 vols.* (Not sold separately.)

Seneca. A Selection. By HERBERT C. SIDLEY.

Emerson's Conduct of Life.

Light from the East. Selections from the Teaching of the Buddha. By EDITH WARD. With Foreword by ANNIE BESANT.

Mathematical Law in the Spiritual World. By EUSTACE MILES.

Better Food for Boys. By EUSTACE MILES, author of "Muscle, Brain, and Diet."

Parables from Nature. A Selection. By Mrs A. GATTY. *6th Thousand.*

Billy and Hans: My Squirrel Friends. A True History. By W. J. STILLMAN.

Neptune the Wise. Episodes in his Life. By C. J.

Friends of Mine: A Book for Animal Lovers. By Mrs M. CORBET SEYMOUR.

Kith and Kin: Poems of Animal Life, selected by HENRY S. SALT, author of "Animals' Rights."

Legends and Lyrics. By ADELAIDE ·A. PROCTER. First Series. *130th Thousand.*

Legends and Lyrics. Second Series. *104th Thousand.*

Aurora Leigh. By Mrs BROWNING.

Tennyson's In Memoriam.

OTHERS TO FOLLOW

LONDON : GEORGE BELL & SONS
YORK HOUSE, PORTUGAL STREET, LINCOLN'S INN, E.C.

BELL'S
INDIAN & COLONIAL LIBRARY.

Issued for Circulation in India and the Colonies only.

PAPER COVERS, 2s. 6d. EACH.   CLOTH, 3s. 6d. EACH.

Additional Volumes are issued at regular intervals.

Calverley (C. S.).
  Verses and Fly-Leaves (14).
  Complete Works (472).
Capes (Bernard).
  Joan Brotherhood (345).
  A Castle in Spain (474).
  The Secret in the Hill (523).
Chesterton (Gilbert K.).
  The Club of Queer Trades.
Childers (Erskine).
  The Riddle of the Sands (494).
Cleeve (Lucas).
  The Man in the Street (470).
  From Crown to Cross (495).
  Anglo-Americans (501).
  Children of Endurance (580).
Cobb (Thomas).
  The Intriguers (478).
Cobban (J. M.).
  The Golden Tooth (377).
Coleridge (Christabel).
  The Winds of Cathrigg (414).
Conrad (Joseph).
  Nostromo (582).
**Conrad (Joseph) and Hueffer
  (Ford Madox).**
  Romance (521).
Crane (Stephen).
  Great Battles of the World (390).
  Last Words (433).
Creswick (Paul).
  At the Sign of the Cross Keys
  (328).
Crockett (S. R.).
  The Men of the Moss-Hags (91).
Croker (B. M.).
  Her Own People (518).
Cullum (Ridgwell).
  The Hound from the North (575)
Cushing (Paul).
  God's Lad (352).
Davidson (L. C.).
  The Theft of a Heart (428).
Dawe (W. Carlton).
  The Prime Minister (507).
Dearmer (Mabel).
  The Orangery (552).
De la Pasture (Mrs. Henry).
  Deborah of Tod's (211).
  Adam Grigson (290).
  Catherine of Calais (388).
  Cornelius (482).

De la Pasture (Mrs. Henry).
  Peter's Mother.
Donovan (Dick).
  Jim the Penman (421).
Douglas (George).
  The House with the Green
  Shutters (417).
Douglas (Theo.).
  A Legacy of Hate (286).
  Nemo (309).
Doyle (A. Conan).
  The White Company (20).
  Rodney Stone. Illus. (143).
  Uncle Bernac. Illus. (168).
  The Tragedy of the Korosko
  (204).
  The Green Flag, &c. (313).
  The Great Boer War (349).
  The War in S. Africa. (Paper
  covers only, 6d.)
Du Maurier (G.).
  Trilby. Illustrated (65).
  The Martian. Illustrated (180).
Ebers (Georg).
  An Egyptian Princess (2).
Falkner (J. Meade).
  Moonfleet (260).
Fenn (G. Manville).
  It Came to Pass (499).
  Coming Home to Roost (558).
  Trapper Dan.
Finnemore (John).
  The Red Men of the Dusk (295).
  The Lover Fugitives (427).
Fitchett (W. H.), LL.D.
  Deeds that Won the Empire.
  Illustrated (198).
  Fights for the Flag. Illus. (248).
  How England Saved Europe.
  4 vols. Illustrated (323–326).
  Wellington's Men (358).
  The Tale of the Great Mutiny
  (412).
  Nelson and his Captains (467).
  Commander of the Hirondelle
  (574).
Fletcher (J. S.).
  Bonds of Steel (429).
Francis (M. E.).
  North, South, and over the Sea
  (447).

AN ALPHABETICAL LIST OF THE BOOKS CONTAINED IN BOHN'S LIBRARIES.

780 Volumes, Small Post 8vo. cloth. Price £165 17s. 6d.

Complete Detailed Catalogue will be sent on application.

Addison's Works. 6 vols. 3*s*. 6*d*. each.

Aeschylus. Verse Trans. by Anna Swanwick. 5*s*.
—— Prose Trans. by T. A. Buckley. 3*s*. 6*d*.

Agassiz & Gould's Comparative Physiology. 5*s*.

Alfieri's Tragedies. Trans. by Bowring. 2 vols. 3*s*. 6*d*. each.

Alford's Queen's English. 1*s*. and 1*s*. 6*d*.

Allen's Battles of the British Navy. 2 vols. 5*s*. each.

Ammianus Marcellinus. Trans. by C. D. Yonge. 7*s*. 6*d*.

Andersen's Danish Tales. Trans. by Caroline Peachey. 5*s*.

Antoninus (Marcus Aurelius). Trans. by George Long. 3*s*. 6*d*.

Apollonius Rhodius. The Argonautica. Trans. by E. P. Coleridge. 5*s*.

Appian's Roman History. Trans. by Horace White. 2 vols. 6*s*. each.

Apuleius, The Works of. 5*s*.

Ariosto's Orlando Furioso. Trans. by W. S. Rose. 2 vols. 5*s*. each.

Aristophanes. Trans. by W. J. Hickie. 2 vols. 5*s*. each.

Aristotle's Works. 5 vols. 5*s*. each; 2 vols. 3*s*. 6*d*. each.

Arrian's Anabasis. Trans. by E. J. Chinnock. 5*s*.

Ascham's Scholemaster. (J. E. B. Mayor.) 1*s*.

Bacon's Essays and Historical Works, 3*s*. 6*d*.; Essays, 1*s*. and 1*s*. 6*d*.; Novum Organum, and Advancement of Learning, 5*s*.

Ballads and Songs of the Peasantry By Robert Bell. 3*s*. 6*d*.

Bass's Lexicon to the Greek Test. 2*s*.

Bax's Manual of the History of Philosophy. 5*s*.

Beaumont and Fletcher. Leigh Hunt's Selections. 3*s*. 6*d*.

Bechstein's Cage and Chamber Birds. 5*s*.

Bede's Ecclesiastical History and the A.S. Chronicle. 5*s*.

Bell (Sir C.) On the Hand. 5*s*.
—— Anatomy of Expression. 5*s*.

Bentley's Phalaris. 5*s*.

Berkeley's Works. (Sampson.) With Introduction by Right Hon. A. J. Balfour, M.P. 3 vols. 5*s*. each.

Björnson's Arne and The Fisher Lassie. Trans. by W. H. Low. 3*s*. 6*d*.

Blair's Chronological Tables. 10*s* Index of Dates. 2 vols. 5*s*. each.

Bleek's Introduction to the Old Testament. 2 vols. 5*s*. each.

Boethius' Consolation of Philosophy &c. 5*s*.

Bohn's Dictionary of Poetical Quotations. 6*s*.

Bond's Handy Book for Verifying Dates, &c. 5*s*.

Bonomi's Nineveh. 5*s*.

Boswell's Life of Johnson. (Napier.) 6 vols. 3*s*. 6*d*. each.

Brand's Popular Antiquities. 3 vols. 5*s*. each.

Bremer's Works. Trans. by Mary Howitt. 4 vols. 3*s*. 6*d*. each.

Bridgewater Treatises. 9 vols. Various prices.

Brink (B. Ten). Early English Literature. 3 vols. 3s. 6d. each.

—— Five Lectures on Shakespeare. 3s. 6d.

Browne's (Sir Thomas) Works. 3 vols. 3s. 6d. each.

Buchanan's Dictionary of Scientific Terms. 6s.

Buckland's Geology and Mineralogy. 2 vols. 15s.

Burke's Works and Speeches. 8 vols. 3s. 6d. each. The Sublime and Beautiful. 1s. and 1s. 6d. Reflections on the French Revolution. 1s.

—— Life, by Sir James Prior. 3s. 6d.

Burney's Evelina. 3s. 6d. Cecilia. 2 vols. 3s. 6d. each.

Burns' Life by Lockhart. Revised by W. Scott Douglas. 3s. 6d.

Burn's Ancient Rome. 7s. 6d.

Burton's Anatomy of Melancholy. A. R. Shilleto.) 3 vols. 3s. 6d. each.

Burton's Pilgrimage to Al-Madinah and Meccah. 2 vols. 3s. 6d. each.

Butler's Analogy of Religion, and Sermons. 3s. 6d.

Butler's Hudibras. 5s.; or 2 vols., 5s. each.

Caesar. Tran. by W. A. M'Devitte. 5s.

Camoens' Lusiad. Mickle's Translation, revised. 3s. 6d.

Carafas (The) of Maddaloni. By Alfred de Reumont. 3s. 6d.

Carlyle's Sartor Resartus. Illustrated by E. J. Sullivan. 5s.

Carpenter's Mechanical Philosophy, 5s. Vegetable Physiology, 6s. Animal Physiology, 6s.

Carrel's Counter Revolution under Charles II. and James II. 3s. 6d.

Cattermole's Evenings at Haddon Hall. 5s.

Catullus and Tibullus. Trans. by W. K. Kelly. 5s.

Cellini's Memoirs. (Roscoe.) 3s. 6d.

Cervantes' Exemplary Novels. Trans. by W. K. Kelly. 3s. 6d.

Cervantes' Don Quixote. Motteux's Trans. revised. 2 vols. 3s. 6d. each.

—— Galatea. Trans. by G. W. J. Gyll. 3s. 6d.

Chalmers On Man. 5s.

Channing's The Perfect Life. 1s. and 1s. 6d.

Chaucer's Works. Bell's Edition, revised by Skeat. 4 vols. 3s. 6d. each.

Chess Congress of 1862. By J. Löwenthal. 5s.

Chevreul on Colour. 5s. and 7s. 6d.

Chillingworth's The Religion of Protestants. 3s. 6d.

China: Pictorial, Descriptive, and Historical. 5s.

Chronicles of the Crusades. 5s.

Cicero's Works. Trans. by Prof. C. D. Yonge and others. 7 vols. 5s. each. 1 vol., 3s. 6d.

—— Letters. Trans. by E. S. Shuckburgh, M.A. 4 vols. 5s. each.

—— Friendship and Old Age. 1s. and 1s. 6d.

Clark's Heraldry. (Planché.) 5s. and 15s.

Classic Tales. 3s. 6d.

Coleridge's Prose Works. (Ashe.) 6 vols. 3s. 6d. each.

Comte's Philosophy of the Sciences. (G. H. Lewes.) 5s.

—— Positive Philosophy. (Harriet Martineau.) 3 vols. 5s. each.

Condé's History of the Arabs in Spain. 3 vols. 3s. 6d. each.

Cooper's Biographical Dictionary. 2 vols. 5s. each.

Coxe's House of Austria. 4 vols. 3s. 6d. each. Memoirs of Marlborough. 3 vols. 3s. 6d. each. Atlas to Marlborough's Campaigns. 10s. 6d.

Craik's Pursuit of Knowledge. 5s.

Craven's Young Sportsman's Manual. 5s.

Cruikshank's Punch and Judy. 5s. Three Courses and a Desert. 5s.

Cunningham's Lives of British Painters. 3 vols. 3s. 6d. each.

Dante. Trans. by Rev. H. F. Cary. 3*s*. 6*d*. Inferno. Separate, 1*s*. and 1*s*. 6*d*. Purgatorio. 1*s*. and 1*s*. 6*d*. Paradiso. 1*s*. and 1*s*. 6*d*.
—— Trans. by I. C. Wright. (Flaxman's Illustrations.) 5*s*.
—— Inferno. Italian Text and Trans. by Dr. Carlyle. 5*s*.
—— Purgatorio. Italian Text and Trans. by W. S. Dugdale. 5*s*.

De Commines' Memoirs. Trans. by A. R. Scoble. 2 vols. 3*s*. 6*d*. each.

Defoe's Novels and Miscel. Works. 6 vols. 3*s*. 6*d*. each. Robinson Crusoe (Vol. VII.) 3*s*. 6*d*. or 5*s*. The Plague in London. 1*s*. and 1*s*. 6*d*.

Delolme on the Constitution of England. 3*s*. 6*d*.

Demmin's Arms and Armour. Trans. by C. C. Black. 7*s*. 6*d*.

Demosthenes' Orations. Trans. by C. Rann Kennedy. 4 vols. 5*s*., and 1 vol. 3*s*. 6*d*.
—— Orations On the Crown. 1*s*. and 1*s*. 6*d*.

De Stael's Corinne. Trans. by Emily Baldwin and Paulina Driver. 3*s*. 6*d*.

Devey's Logic. 5*s*.

Dictionary of Greek and Latin Quotations. 5*s*.
—— of Poetical Quotations (Bohn). 6*s*.
—— of Scientific Terms. (Buchanan.) 6*s*.
—— of Biography. (Cooper.) 2 vols. 5*s*. each.
—— of Noted Names o Fiction. (Wheeler.) 5*s*.
—— Of Obsolete and Provincial English. (Wright.) 2 vols. 5*s*. each.

Didron's Christian Iconography. 2 vols. 5*s*. each.

Diogenes Laertius. Trans. by C. D. Yonge. 5*s*.

Dobree's Adversaria. (Wagner.) (2 vols.) 5*s*. each.

Dodd's Epigrammatists. 6*s*.

Donaldson's Theatre of the Greeks. 5*s*.

Draper's History of the Intellectual Development of Europe. 2 vols. 5*s*. each.

Dunlop's History of Fiction. 2 vols. 5*s*. each.

Dyer's History of Pompeii.
—— The City of Rome. 5*s*.

Dyer's British Popular Customs. 5*s*.

Eaton's Waterloo Days. 1*s*. and 1*s*. 6*d*.

Ebers' Egyptian Princess. Trans. by E. S. Buchheim. 3*s*. 6*d*.

Edgeworth's Stories for Children. 3*s*. 6*d*.

Ellis' Specimens of Early English Metrical Romances. (Halliwell.) 5*s*.

Elze's Life of Shakespeare. Trans. by L. Dora Schmitz. 5*s*.

Emerson's Works. 3 vols. 3*s*. 6*d*. each, or 5 vols. 1*s*. each.

Ennemoser's History of Magic. 2 vols. 5*s*. each.

Epictetus. Trans. by George Long. 5*s*.

Euripides. Trans. by E. P. Coleridge. 2 vols. 5*s*. each.

Eusebius' Eccl. History. Trans. by C. F. Cruse. 5*s*.

Evelyn's Diary and Correspondence. (Bray.) 4 vols. 5*s*. each.

Fairholt's Costume in England. (Dillon.) 2 vols. 5*s*. each.

Fielding's Joseph Andrews. 3*s*. 6*d*. Tom Jones. 2 vols. 3*s*. 6*d*. each. Amelia. 5*s*.

Flaxman's Lectures on Sculpture. 6*s*.

Florence of Worcester's Chronicle. Trans. by T. Forester. 5*s*.

Foster's Works. 10 vols. 3*s*. 6*d*. each.

Franklin's Autobiography. 1*s*.

Gaspary's Italian Literature, to the death of Dante. Trans. by H. Oelsner, M.A., Ph.D. 3*s*. 6*d*.

Gesta Romanorum. Trans. by Swan and Hooper. 5*s*.

Gibbon's Decline and Fall. 7 vols. 3*s*. 6*d*. each.

Gilbart's Banking. 2 vols. 5*s*. each.

Gil Blas. Trans. by Smollett. 6*s*.

Giraldus Cambrensis. 5s.

Goethe's Works and Correspondence, including Autobiography and Annals, Faust, Elective Affinities, Werther, Wilhelm Meister, Poems and Ballads, Dramas, Reinecke Fox, Tour in Italy and Miscellaneous Travels, Early and Miscellaneous Letters, Correspondence with Eckermann and Soret, Zelter and Schiller, &c., &c. By various Translators. 16 vols. 3s. 6d. each.

—— Faust. Text with Hayward's Translation. (Buchheim.) 5s.

—— Faust. Part I. Trans. by Anna Swanwick. 1s. and 1s. 6d.

—— Boyhood. (Part I. of the Autobiography.) Trans. by J. Oxenford. 1s. and 1s. 6d.

—— Reinecke Fox. Trans. by A. Rogers. 1s. and 1s. 6d.

Goldsmith's Works. (Gibbs.) 5 vols. 3s. 6d. each.

—— Plays. 1s. and 1s. 6d. Vicar of Wakefield. 1s. and 1s. 6d.

Grammont's Memoirs and Boscobel Tracts. 5s.

Gray's Letters. (D. C. Tovey.) Vols. I. and II. 3s. 6d. each.

Greek Anthology. Trans. by E. Burges. 5s.

Greek Romances. (Theagenes and Chariclea, Daphnis and Chloe, Clitopho and Leucippe.) Trans. by Rev. R. Smith. 5s.

Greek Testament. 5s.

Greene, Marlowe, and Ben Jonson's Poems. (Robert Bell.) 3s. 6d.

Gregory's Evidences of the Christian Religion. 3s. 6d.

Grimm's Gammer Grethel. Trans. by E. Taylor. 3s. 6d.

—— German Tales. Trans. by Mrs. Hunt. 2 vols. 3s. 6d. each.

Grossi's Marco Visconti. 3s. 6d.

Guizot's The English Revolution of 1640. Trans. by W. Hazlitt. 3s. 6d.

—— History of Civilisation. Trans. by W. Hazlitt. 3 vols. 3s. 6d. each.

Hall (Robert). Miscellaneous Works. 3s. 6d.

Hampton Court. A Short History of the Manor and Palace. By Ernest Law, B.A. 5s.

Handbooks of Athletic Sports. 8 vols. 3s. 6d. each.

Handbook of Card and Table Games. 2 vols. 3s. 6d. each.

—— of Proverbs. By H. G. Bohn. 5s.

—— of Foreign Proverbs. 5s.

Hardwick's History of the Thirty-nine Articles. 5s.

Harvey's Circulation of the Blood (Bowie.) 1s. and 1s. 6d.

Hauff's Tales. Trans. by S. Mendel. 3s. 6d.

—— The Caravan and Sheik of Alexandria. 1s. and 1s. 6d.

Hawthorne's Novels and Tales. 4 vols. 3s. 6d. each.

Hazlitt's Lectures and Essays. 7 vols. 3s. 6d. each.

Heaton's History of Painting. (Cosmo Monkhouse.) 5s.

Hegel's Philosophy of History. Trans. by J. Sibree. 5s.

Heine's Poems. Trans. by E. A. Bowring. 3s. 6d.

—— Travel Pictures. Trans. by Francis Storr. 3s. 6d.

Helps (Sir Arthur). Life of Columbus. 3s. 6d.

—— Life of Pizarro. 3s. 6d.

—— Life of Cortes. 2 vols. 3s. 6d. each.

—— Life of Las Casas. 3s. 6d.

—— Life of Thomas Brassey. 1s. and 1s. 6d.

Henderson's Historical Documents of the Middle Ages. 5s.

Henfrey's English Coins. (Keary.) 6s.

Henry (Matthew) On the Psalms. 5s.

Henry of Huntingdon's History. Trans. by T. Forester. 5s.

Herodotus. Trans. by H. F. Cary. 3s. 6d.

—— Wheeler's Analysis and Summary of. 5s. Turner's Notes on. 5s.

Hesiod, Callimachus and Theognis. Trans. by Rev. J. Banks. 5*s.*

Hoffmann's Tales. The Serapion Brethren. Trans. by Lieut.-Colonel Ewing. 2 vols. 3*s. 6d.*

Hogg's Experimental and Natural Philosophy. 5*s.*

Holbein's Dance of Death and Bible Cuts. 5*s.*

Homer. Trans. by T. A. Buckley. 2 vols. 5*s.* each.

Hooper's Waterloo. 3*s. 6d.*

—— Sedan. 3*s. 6d*

Horace. A New Literal Prose Translation. By A. Hamilton Bryce, LL.D. 3*s. 6d.*

Hugo's Dramatic Works. Trans. by Mrs. Crosland and F. L. Slous. 3*s. 6d.*

—— Hernani. Trans. by Mrs. Crosland. 1*s.*

—— Poems. Trans. by various writers. Collected by J. H. L. Williams. 3*s. 6d.*

Humboldt's Cosmos. Trans. by Otté, Paul, and Dallas. 4 vols. 3*s. 6d.* each, and 1 vol. 5*s.*

—— Personal Narrative of his Travels. Trans. by T. Ross. 3 vols. 5*s.* each.

—— Views of Nature. Trans. by Otté and Bohn. 5*s.*

Humphreys' Coin Collector's Manual. 2 vols. 5*s.* each.

Hungary, History of. 3*s. 6d.*

Hunt's Poetry of Science. 5*s.*

Hutchinson's Memoirs. 3*s. 6d.*

India before the Sepoy Mutiny. 5*s.*

Ingulph's Chronicles. 5*s.*

Irving (Washington). Complete Works. 15 vols. 3*s. 6d.* each; or in 18 vols. 1*s.* each, and 2 vols. 1*s. 6d.* each.

—— Life and Letters. By Pierre E. Irving. 2 vols. 3*s. 6d.* each.

Isocrates. Trans. by J. H. Freese. Vol. I. 5*s.*

James' Life of Richard Cœur de Lion. 2 vols. 3*s. 6d.* each.

—— Life and Times of Louis XIV. 2 vols. 3*s. 6d.* each.

Jameson (Mrs.) Shakespeare's Heroines. 3*s. 6d.*

Jesse (E.) Anecdotes of Dogs. 5*s.*

Jesse (J. H.) Memoirs of the Court of England under the Stuarts. 3 vols. 5*s.* each.

—— Memoirs of the Pretenders. 5*s.*

Johnson's Lives of the Poets. (Napier.) 3 vols. 3*s. 6d.* each.

Josephus. Whiston's Translation, revised by Rev. A. R. Shilleto. 5 vols. 3*s. 6d.* each.

Joyce's Scientific Dialogues. 5*s.*

Jukes-Browne's Handbook of Physical Geology. 7*s. 6d.* Handbook of Historical Geology. 6*s.* The Building of the British Isles. 7*s. 6d.*

Julian the Emperor. Trans. by Rev. C. W. King. 5*s.*

Junius's Letters. Woodfall's Edition, revised. 2 vols. 3*s. 6d.* each.

Justin, Cornelius Nepos, and Eutropius. Trans. by Rev. J. S. Watson. 5*s.*

Juvenal, Persius, Sulpicia, and Lucilius. Trans. by L. Evans. 5*s.*

Kant's Critique of Pure Reason. Trans. by J. M. D. Meiklejohn. 5*s.*

—— Prolegomena, &c. Trans. by E. Belfort Bax. 5*s.*

Keightley's Fairy Mythology. 5*s.* Classical Mythology. Revised by Dr. L. Schmitz. 5*s.*

Kidd On Man. 3*s. 6d.*

Kirby On Animals. 2 vols. 5*s.* each.

Knight's Knowledge is Power. 5*s.*

La Fontaine's Fables. Trans. by E. Wright. 3*s. 6d.*

Lamartine's History of the Girondists. Trans. by H. T. Ryde. 3 vols. 3*s. 6d.* each.

—— Restoration of the Monarchy in France. Trans. by Capt. Rafter. 4 vols. 3*s. 6d.* each.

—— French Revolution of 1848. 3*s. 6d.*

Lamb's Essays of Elia and Eliana. 3*s. 6d.,* or in 3 vols. 1*s.* each.

—— Memorials and Letters. Talfourd's Edition, revised by W. C. Hazlitt. 2 vols. 3*s. 6d.* each.

—— Specimens of the English Dramatic Poets of the Time of Elizabeth. 3*s. 6d.*

—— Tales from Shakespeare. With 24 Illustrations by Byam Shaw. 3*s. 6d.*

Lanzi's History of Painting in Italy. Trans. by T. Roscoe. 3 vols. 3s. 6d. each.

Lappenberg's England under the Anglo-Saxon Kings. Trans. by B. Thorpe. 2 vols. 3s. 6d. each.

Lectures on Painting. By Barry, Opie, and Fuseli. 5s.

Leonardo da Vinci's Treatise on Painting. Trans. by J. F. Rigaud. 5s.

Lepsius' Letters from Egypt, &c. Trans. by L. and J. B. Horner. 5s.

Lessing's Dramatic Works. Trans. by Ernest Bell. 2 vols. 3s. 6d. each. Nathan the Wise and Minna von Barnhelm. 1s. and 1s. 6d. Laokoon, Dramatic Notes, &c. Trans. by E. C. Beasley and Helen Zimmern. 3s. 6d. Laokoon separate. 1s. or 1s. 6d.

Lilly's Introduction to Astrology. (Zadkiel.) 5s.

Livy. Trans. by Dr. Spillan and others. 4 vols. 5s. each.

Locke's Philosophical Works. (J. A. St. John.) 2 vols. 3s. 6d. each.
—— Life. By Lord King. 3s. 6d.

Lodge's Portraits. 8 vols. 5s. each.

Longfellow's Poetical and Prose Works. 2 vols. 5s. each.

Loudon's Natural History. 5s.

Lowndes' Bibliographer's Manual 6 vols. 5s. each.

Lucan's Pharsalia. Trans. by H. T. Riley. 5s.

Lucian's Dialogues. Trans. by H. Williams. 5s.

Lucretius. Trans. by Rev. J. S. Watson. 5s.

Luther's Table Talk. Trans. by W. Hazlitt. 3s. 6d.
—— Autobiography. (Michelet.) Trans. by W. Hazlitt. 3s. 6d.

Machiavelli's History of Florence, &c. Trans. 3s. 6d.

Mallet's Northern Antiquities. 5s.

Mantell's Geological Excursions through the Isle of Wight, &c. 5s. Petrifactions and their Teachings. 6s. Wonders of Geology. 2 vols. 7s. 6d. each.

Manzoni's The Betrothed. 5s.

Marco Polo's Travels. Marsden's Edition, revised by T. Wright. 5s.

Martial's Epigrams. Trans. 7s. 6d.

Martineau's History of England, 1800–15. 3s. 6d.
—— History of the Peace, 1816–46. 4 vols. 3s. 6d. each.

Matthew Paris. Trans. by Dr. Giles. 3 vols. 5s. each.

Matthew of Westminster. Trans. by C. D. Yonge. 2 vols. 5s. each.

Maxwell's Victories of Wellington. 5s.

Menzel's History of Germany. Trans. by Mrs. Horrocks. 3 vols. 3s. 6d. ea.

Michael Angelo and Raffaelle. By Duppa and Q. de Quincy. 5s.

Michelet's French Revolution. Trans. by C. Cocks. 3s. 6d.

Mignet's French Revolution. 3s. 6d.

Mill (John Stuart). Early Essays. 3s. 6d.

Miller's Philosophy of History. 4 vols. 3s. 6d. each.

Milton's Poetical Works. (J. Montgomery.) 2 vols. 3s. 6d. each.
—— Prose Works. (J. A. St. John.) 5 vols. 3s. 6d. each.

Mitford's Our Village. 2 vols. 3s. 6d. each.

Molière's Dramatic Works. Trans. by C. H. Wall. 3 vols. 3s. 6d. each.
—— The Miser, Tartuffe, The Shopkeeper turned Gentlemen. 1s. & 1s. 6d.

Montagu's (Lady M. W.) Letters and Works. (Wharncliffe and Moy Thomas.) 2 vols. 5s. each.

Montaigne's Essays. Cotton's Trans. revised by W. C. Hazlitt. 3 vols. 3s. 6d. each.

Montesquieu's Spirit of Laws. Nugent's Trans. revised by J. V Prichard. 2 vols. 3s. 6d. each.

Morphy's Games of Chess. (Löwenthal.) 5s.

Motley's Dutch Republic. 3 vols. 3s. 6d. each.

Mudie's British Birds. (Martin.) 2 vols. 5s. each.

Naval and Military Heroes of Great Britain. 6s.

Neander's History of the Christian Religion and Church. 10 vols. Life of Christ. 1 vol. Planting and Training of the Church by the Apostles. 2 vols. History of Christian Dogma. 2 vols. Memorials of Christian Life in the Early and Middle Ages. 16 vols. 3s. 6d. each.

Nibelungs, Lay of the. Trans. by Alice Horton and Edward Bell, M.A. 5s.

Nicolini's History of the Jesuits. 5s.

North's Lives of the Norths. (Jessopp.) 3 vols. 3s. 6d. each.

Nugent's Memorials of Hampden. 5s.

Ockley's History of the Saracens. 3s. 6d.

Oman (J. C.) The Great Italian Epics. 3s. 6d.

Ordericus Vitalis. Trans. by T Forester. 4 vols. 5s. each.

Ovid. Trans. by H. T. Riley. 3 vols. 5s. each.

Pascal's Thoughts. Trans. by C. Kegan Paul. 3s. 6d.

Pauli's Life of Alfred the Great, &c. 5s.

—— Life of Cromwell. 1s. and 1s. 6d.

Pausanias' Description of Greece. Trans. by Rev. A. R. Shilleto. 2 vols. 5s. each.

Pearson on the Creed. (Walford.) 5s.

Pepys' Diary. (Braybrooke.) 4 vols. 5s. each.

Percy's Reliques of Ancient English Poetry. (Prichard.) 2 vols. 3s. 6d. ea.

Petrarch's Sonnets. 5s.

Pettigrew's Chronicles of the Tombs. 5s.

Philo-Judæus. Trans. by C. D. Yonge. 4 vols. 5s. each.

Pickering's Races of Man. 5s.

Pindar. Trans. by D. W. Turner. 5s.

Planché's History of British Costume. 5s.

Plato. Trans. by H. Cary, G. Burges, and H. Davis. 6 vols. 5s. each.

—— Apology, Crito, Phædo, Protagoras. 1s. and 1s. 6d.

—— Day's Analysis and Index to the Dialogues. 5s.

Plautus. Trans. by H. T. Riley. 2 vols. 5s. each.

—— Trinummus, Menæchmi, Aulularia, Captivi. 1s. and 1s. 6d.

Pliny's Natural History. Trans. by Dr. Bostock and H. T. Riley. 6 vols. 5s. each.

Pliny the Younger, Letters of. Melmoth's trans. revised by Rev. F. C. T. Bosanquet. 5s.

Plotinus: Select Works of. Tom Taylor's trans. (G. R. S. Mead.) 5s.

Plutarch's Lives. Trans. by Stewart and Long. 4 vols. 3s. 6d. each.

—— Moralia. Trans. by Rev. C. W. King and Rev. A. R. Shilleto. 2 vols. 5s. each.

Poetry of America. (W. J. Linton.) 3s. 6d.

Political Cyclopædia. 4 vols. 3s. 6d. each.

Polyglot of Foreign Proverbs. 5s.

Pope's Poetical Works. (Carruthers.) 2 vols. 5s. each.

—— Homer. (J. S. Watson. 2 vols. 5s. each.

—— Life and Letters. (Carruthers.) 5s.

Pottery and Porcelain. (H. G. Bohn. 5s. and 10s. 6d.

Poushkin's Prose Tales. Trans. by T. Keane. 3s. 6d.

Prescott's Conquest of Mexico. (J. F. Kirk). With an Introduction by George Parker Winship. 3 vols. 3s. 6d. each.

—— Conquest of Peru. (J. F. Kirk. 2 vols. 3s. 6d. each.

—— Ferdinand and Isabella. (J. F. Kirk.) 3 vols. 3s. 6d. each.

Propertius. Trans. by Rev. P. J. F. Gantillon. 3s. 6d.

Prout (Father). Reliques. 5s.

Quintilian's Institutes of Oratory. Trans. by Rev. J. S. Watson. 2 vols. 5s. each.

Racine's Tragedies. Trans. by R. B. Boswell. 2 vols. 3s. 6d. each.

Ranke's History of the Popes. Trans. by E. Foster. 3 vols. 3s. 6d. each.

—— History of Servia. Trans. by Mrs. Kerr. 3s. 6d.

Rennie's Insect Architecture. (J. G. Wood.) 5s.

Reynolds' Discourses and Essays (Beechy.) 2 vols. 3*s*. 6*d*. each.

Ricardo's Political Economy. (Gonner.) 5*s*.

Richter's Levana. 3*s*. 6*d*.
—— Flower Fruit and Thorn Pieces. Trans. by Lieut.-Col. Ewing. 3*s*. 6*d*.

Roger de Hovenden's Annals. Trans. by Dr. Giles. 2 vols. 5*s*. each.

Roger of Wendover. Trans. by Dr. Giles. 2 vols. 5*s*. each.

Roget's Animal and Vegetable Physiology. 2 vols. 6*s*. each.

Rome in the Nineteenth Century. (C. A. Eaton.) 2 vols. 5*s*. each.

Roscoe's Leo X. 2 vols. 3*s*. 6*d*. each.
—— Lorenzo de' Medici. 3*s*. 6*d*.

Russia, History of. By W. K. Kelly. 2 vols. 3*s*. 6*d*. each.

Sallust, Florus, and Velleius Paterculus. Trans. by Rev. J. S. Watson. 5*s*.

Schiller's Works. Including History of the Thirty Years' War, Revolt of the Netherlands, Wallenstein, William Tell, Don Carlos, Mary Stuart, Maid of Orleans, Bride of Messina, Robbers, Fiesco, Love and Intrigue, Demetrius, Ghost-Seer, Sport of Divinity, Poems, Aesthetical and Philosophical Essays, &c. By various translators. 7 vols. 3*s*. 6*d*. each.
—— Mary Stuart and The Maid of Orleans. Trans. by J. Mellish and Anna Swanwick. 1*s*. and 1*s*. 6*d*.

Schlegel's (F.) Lectures and Miscellaneous Works. 5 vols. 3*s*. 6*d*. each.
—— **(A. W.)** Lectures on Dramatic Art and Literature. 3*s*. 6*d*.

Schopenhauer's Essays. Selected and trans. by E. Belfort Bax. 5*s*.
—— On the Fourfold Root of the Principle of Sufficient Reason and on the Will in Nature. Trans. by Mdme. Hillebrand. 5*s*.

Schouw's Earth, Plants, and Man. Trans. by A. Henfrey. 5*s*.

Schumann's Early Letters. Trans. by May Herbert. 3*s*. 6*d*.
—— Reissmann's Life of. Trans. by A. L. Alger. 3*s*. 6*d*.

Seneca on Benefits. Trans. by Aubrey Stewart. 3*s*. 6*d*.
—— Minor Essays and On Clemency. Trans. by Aubrey Stewart. 5*s*.

Sharpe's History of Egypt. 2 vols. 5*s*. each.

Shakespeare's Documents. Arranged by D. H. Lambert, B.A. 3*s*. 6*d*.

Sheridan's Dramatic Works. 3*s*. 6*d*.
—— Plays. 1*s*. and 1*s*. 6*d*.

Sismondi's Literature of the South of Europe. Trans. by T. Roscoe. 2 vols. 3*s*. 6*d*. each.

Six Old English Chronicles. 5*s*.

Smith (Archdeacon). Synonyms and Antonyms. 5*s*.
—— Synonyms Discriminated. 6*s*.

Smith (Adam). Wealth of Nations. (Belfort Bax.) 2 vols. 3*s*. 6*d*. each.
—— Theory of Moral Sentiments. 3*s*. 6*d*.

Smith (Pye). Geology and Scripture. 5*s*.

Smollett's Novels. 4 vols. 3*s*. 6*d*. each.

Smyth's Lectures on Modern History. 2 vols. 3*s*. 6*d*. each.

Socrates' Ecclesiastical History. 5*s*.

Sophocles. Trans. by E. P. Coleridge, M.A. 5*s*.

Southey's Life of Nelson. 5*s*.
—— Life of Wesley. 5*s*.
—— Life, as told in his Letters. By J. Dennis. 3*s*. 6*d*.

Sozomen's Ecclesiastical History. 5*s*.

Spinoza's Chief Works. Trans. by R. H. M. Elwes. 2 vols. 5*s*. each.

Stanley's Dutch and Flemish Painters. 5*s*.

Starling's Noble Deeds of Women. 5*s*.

Staunton's Chess Player's Handbook. 5*s*. Chess Praxis. 5*s*. Chess Players' Companion. 5*s*. Chess Tournament of 1851. 5*s*.

Stöckhardt's Experimental Chemistry (Heaton.) 5*s*.

Strabo's Geography. Trans. by Falconer and Hamilton. 3 vols. 5*s*. each.

Strickland's Queens of England. 6 vols. 5s. each. Mary Queen of Scots. 2 vols. 5s. each. Tudor and Stuart Princesses. 5s.

Stuart & Revett's Antiquities of Athens. 5s.

Suetonius' Lives of the Caesars and of the Grammarians. Thomson's trans. revised by T. Forester. 5s.

Sully's Memoirs. Mrs. Lennox's trans. revised. 4 vols. 3s. 6d. each.

Swift's Prose Works. (Temple Scott.) With Introduction by W. E. H. Lecky. 12 vols. 3s. 6d. each.
[*Vols.* 1-6, 8-10 *ready.*

Tacitus. The Oxford trans. revised. 2 vols. 5s. each.

Tales of the Genii. **Trans. by** Sir Charles Morell. 5s.

Tasso's Jerusalem Delivered. Trans. by J. H. Wiffen. 5s.

Taylor's Holy Living and Holy Dying. 3s. 6d.

Terence and Phædrus. Trans. by H. T. Riley. 5s.

Theocritus, Bion, Moschus, and Tyrtæus. Trans. by Rev. J. Banks. 5s.

Theodoret and Evagrius. 5s.

Thierry's Norman Conquest. Trans. by W. Hazlitt. 2 vols. 3s. 6d. each.

Thucydides. Trans. by Rev. H. Dale. 2 vols. 3s. 6d. each.

—— Wheeler's Analysis and Summary of. 5s.

Thudichum's Treatise on Wines. 5s.

Trevelyan's Ladies in Parliament. 1s. and 1s. 6d.

Ulrici's Shakespeare's Dramatic Art. Trans. by L. Dora Schmitz. 2 vols. 3s. 6d. each.

Uncle Tom's Cabin. 3s. 6d.

Ure's Cotton Manufacture of Great Britain. 2 vols. 5s. each.

—— Philosophy of Manufacture. 7s. 6d.

Vasari's Lives of the Painters. Trans. by Mrs. Foster. 6 vols. 3s. 6d. each.

Virgil. Trans. by A. Hamilton Bryce, LL.D. 3s. 6d.

Voltaire's Tales. Trans. by R. B. Boswell. 3s. 6d.

Walton's Angler. 5s.

—— Lives. (A. H. Bullen.) 5s.

Waterloo Days. By C. A. Eaton. 1s. and 1s. 6d.

Wellington, Life of. By 'An Old Soldier.' 5s.

Werner's Templars in Cyprus. Trans. by E. A. M. Lewis. 3s. 6d.

Westropp's Handbook of Archæology. 5s.

Wheatley. On the Book of Common Prayer. 3s. 6d.

Wheeler's Dictionary of Noted Names of Fiction. 5s.

White's Natural History of Selborne. 5s.

Wieseler's Synopsis of the Gospels. 5s.

William of Malmesbury's Chronicle. 5s.

Wright's Dictionary of Obsolete and Provincial English. 2 vols. 5s. each.

Xenophon. Trans. by Rev. J. S. Watson and Rev. H. Dale. 3 vols. 5s. each.

Young's Travels in France, 1787-89. (M. Betham-Edwards.) 3s. 6d.

—— Tour in Ireland, 1776-9. (A. W. Hutton.) 2 vols. 3s. 6d. each.

Yule-Tide Stories. (B. Thorpe.) 5s.

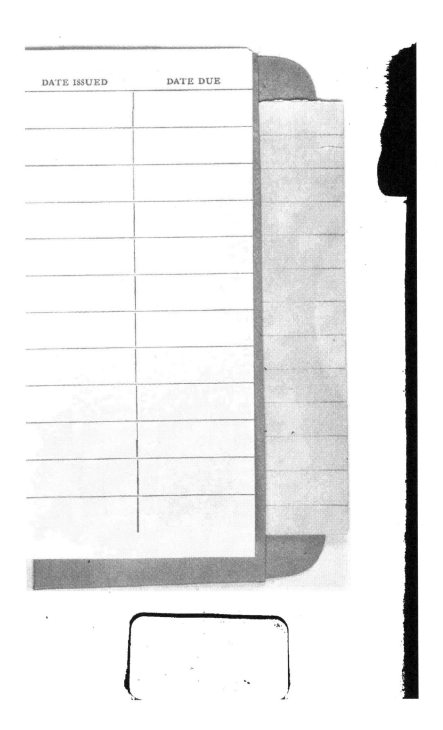

DATE ISSUED	DATE DUE

DATE ISSUED	DATE DUE

32101 066120161

32101 066120161

www.ingramcontent.com/pod-product-compliance
Lightning Source LLC
LaVergne TN
LVHW012204040326
832903LV00003B/116